BILLY GRAHAM

BILLY GRAHAM

A Biography

Roger Bruns

GREENWOOD BIOGRAPHIES

GREENWOOD PRESS
WESTPORT, CONNECTICUT · LONDON

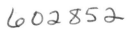

Library of Congress Cataloging-in-Publication Data

Bruns, Roger.
   Billy Graham : a biography / by Roger Bruns.
      p. cm.—(Greenwood biographies, ISSN 1540–4900)
   Includes bibliographical references and index.
   ISBN 0–313–32718–1 (alk. paper)
   1. Graham, Billy, 1918–   2. Evangelists—United States—Biography. I.
Title. II. Series.
BV3785.G69B78   2004
269'.2'092—dc22
[B]   2003060417

British Library Cataloguing in Publication Data is available.

Library of Congress Catalog Card Number: 2003060417
ISBN: 0–313–32718–1
ISSN: 1540–4900

First published in 2004

Greenwood Press, 88 Post Road West, Westport, CT 06881
An imprint of Greenwood Publishing Group, Inc.
www.greenwood.com

Printed in the United States of America

∞

The paper used in this book complies with the
Permanent Paper Standard issued by the National
Information Standards Organization (Z39.48–1984).

10 9 8 7 6 5 4 3 2 1

CONTENTS

Photo essay follows page 74.

SERIES FOREWORD

In response to high school and public library needs, Greenwood developed this distinguished series of full-length biographies specifically for student use. Prepared by field experts and professionals, these engaging biographies are tailored for high school students who need challenging yet accessible biographies. Ideal for secondary school assignments, the length, format, and subject areas are designed to meet educators' requirements and students' interests.

Greenwood offers an extensive selection of biographies spanning all curriculum related subject areas including social studies, the sciences, literature and the arts, and history and politics, as well as popular culture, covering public figures and famous personalities from all time periods and backgrounds, both historic and contemporary, who have made an impact on American and/or world culture. Greenwood biographies were chosen based on comprehensive feedback from librarians and educators. Consideration was given to both curriculum relevance and inherent interest. The result is an intriguing mix of the well known and the unexpected, the saints and the sinners from long-ago history and contemporary pop culture. Readers will find a wide array of subject choices, from fascinating crime figures like Al Capone to inspiring pioneers like Margaret Mead, from the greatest minds of our time like Stephen Hawking to the most amazing success stories of our day like J. K. Rowling.

While the emphasis is on fact, not glorification, the books are meant to be fun to read. Each volume provides in-depth information about the subject's life from birth through childhood, the teen years and adulthood. A thorough account relates family background and education, traces personal and professional influences, and explores struggles, accomplishments, and contributions. A timeline highlights the most significant life events against a historical perspective. Bibliographies supplement the reference value of each volume.

INTRODUCTION

He was a dairy farmer's son from North Carolina who dreamed of becoming a baseball player. Although his talents on the baseball field were middling, he managed in his career to fill stadiums across the country and the world. He was Billy Graham and he was an evangelist.

The magnitude of his accomplishments is unquestioned. In 1957, 100,000 people jammed Yankee Stadium for the closing night of Graham's New York crusade. For 12 weeks, Graham drew an astonishing 2 million listeners in New York City and broke all attendance records for consecutive appearances at historic Madison Square Garden. Wherever he preached, from Chicago to Los Angeles to Washington, the story was the same. He drew the largest crowds ever recorded.

He preached in nearly 200 countries around the world. In London's Wembley Stadium in 1954, Graham spoke to 185,000 individuals who braced themselves against a driving rain to hear the celebrated American evangelist. Attendance at this event topped the crowd at the 1948 Olympics in the same stadium and was the largest religious gathering in British history. In Seoul, Korea, Graham's 1973 crusade drew over one million, the largest recorded religious gathering in history.

With the advent of satellite-link television, the numbers were even more impossible to fathom. In 1990, on his 72nd birthday, Graham preached in Hong Kong. His sermon was broadcast to over 100 million viewers through a network strung across the Asian continent.

Graham and his organization, the Billy Graham Evangelical Association (BGEA), have been a major influence on significant international twentieth-century religious events, especially the International Congress on World Evangelization in Lausanne, Switzerland, in 1974.

He was the first Christian evangelist after the Second World War to hold public religious gatherings behind the Iron Curtain, including controversial visits to the Soviet Union, North Korea, and China.

He personally associated with every American president since Dwight Eisenhower, advising Lyndon Johnson and Richard Nixon on Vietnam and Ronald Reagan on the Soviet Union. Bible in hand, he appeared at the side of President George Bush as the United States launched the 1991 war against Iraq. President George W. Bush credits Graham with leading him out of alcohol abuse to a conversion experience.

His ministry became the center of a post–World War II movement called the new evangelicalism. He played a leading role in developing the nation's two most influential evangelical seminaries, Fuller Theological Seminary in Pasadena, California, and Gordon-Conwell Theological Seminary in Philadelphia, Pennsylvania. His work and his example inspired thousands of young men and women to pursue a career in the ministry.

Graham's magazine, *Decision*, became the most widely distributed religious periodical in the world. His first book, *Peace with God*, published in August 1953, became an immediate bestseller and sold millions. It has been translated into 50 languages. The evangelist has published over 21 books since that time

Through the years, the BGEA headquarters in Minneapolis, Minnesota, received mountains of letters from men, women, and children from all walks of life, an average of over 100,000 a week. Some of the letters bore only the words "Billy Graham, Minneapolis, Minnesota" on the envelopes. No other address was necessary.

Graham has appeared on the Gallup Poll's Ten Most Admired Men list more often than anyone in history. He was listed by *Life* magazine as one of the 100 most important Americans of the twentieth century. In 1971, when he opened a revival in Charlotte, North Carolina, near to his birthplace, town leaders declared a holiday. In a 1978 *Ladies' Home Journal* survey, under the category "achievements in religion," Graham was higher on the list than everyone except God.

His personal finances and that of his organization have been impeccably honest and he has been free of personal scandal. In 1950 he put himself on an annual salary pegged at the level of a successful urban pastor. He has regularly turned down offers to star in movies and to run for political office.

Graham seemed to epitomize middle-class ideals at a time when the postwar American middle class was in its ascendancy. Graham's personality and ideals, his dress and demeanor, and all the sounds and images that were part of his services seemed to many a comfortable call back to basic American values and religious piety.

However, if his accomplishments are unquestioned, there are those who question the truth, influence, and morality of his message.

From both the left and the right of the political and religious spectrums, Graham was attacked. One journalist likened him to a moral dwarf. Atheists and non-Christians labeled his revivals as grotesque circus charades that deceived multitudes of people. Many of the attacks centered on the meaning and techniques of the revivals that Graham had, through efficient organization and the force of his own personality, crafted with such precision and effectiveness. Those revivals sought conversion, the redirecting of one's soul and life under God, an impulse difficult to understand and to influence. Learned scholar Reinhold Niebuhr of New York's Union Seminary ridiculed Graham's sermons as simplistic and charged that the thousands of conversions supposedly achieved by the revivals were sham.[1]

Once Graham made it clear that he would work with anyone who would work with him in his ministry—liberal, Catholic, or even communist—fundamentalist outrage flared. Critics charged Graham with lying about the truths in the Bible, betraying the Christian faith, and committing treasonous actions abroad. They even accused him of allying himself, through ignorance and self-interest, with the devil.

Bob Jones, founder of the college Graham first attended, said that the evangelist had done more damage to the cause of Christianity than any other man. When Jones died, his son sent a letter to Graham saying that the evangelist would not be welcome at Jones's funeral.

To many critics, Graham's links with a succession of American presidents is particularly galling and a betrayal of one of the most revered political emblems of American democracy—the separation of church and state. Although his relationships with Presidents John F. Kennedy and Jimmy Carter could be described as politely cool, for all the others there is substantial evidence that he functioned not only as an unofficial chaplain but also, to some extent, as a policy adviser.

To the revival-goers, however, such hostility was irrelevant as they traveled to an arena or a stadium to attend a Billy Graham revival. They knew what to expect. They knew that his old friend George Beverly Shea would be there, singing the beloved revival favorites, such as "How Great Thou Art." They knew that a well-known athlete or movie star would be there, testifying to the saving power of the gospel. They knew that there would be vigorous songs from a massive choir and that the evangelist himself, waving and stabbing the Bible aloft, pacing across the platform, would deliver a blistering sermon with astonishing speed. The inevitable message would be simple and direct—Christ alone offered a lasting solution to the world's problems.

What are we to make of the career of Billy Graham? What are the results of hundreds of crusades launched and millions of dollars spent? How long did the religious commitments last for those who professed their lives to Christ at the revivals? There is really no way to measure. Sociologists, historians, and the Graham organization itself have made various attempts to gauge the permanency of those decisions. The results, however, depend on who is doing the survey and the tools employed. No one knows for certain. However, millions of people spoke with their feet when they marched forward; they spoke with their hearts when they sat down and wrote those letters. What it all says is that Graham, whatever the merit of his message and beliefs, helped ordinary men and women cope with their lives and find hope in the future.

This is his remarkable story.

NOTE

1. Wacker, "Charles Atlas with a Halo," pp. 336–41.

TIMELINE OF EVENTS IN THE LIFE OF BILLY GRAHAM

November 7, 1918	Graham (William Franklin Graham Jr.) is born in Charlotte, North Carolina
June 10, 1920	Future wife Ruth McCue Bell is born in China
1934	Graham has conversion experience at a Mordecai Ham revival in Charlotte, North Carolina
1936	Attends Bob Jones College for one semester
1937	Preaches first sermon at Palatka, Florida
1937	Transfers to Florida Bible Institute
1938	Conducts small revival in Florida
1940	Enrolls at Wheaton College in Illinois and meets Ruth Bell
1940	Graduates from Florida Bible Institute
1943	Graduates from Wheaton College
August 13, 1943	Marries Ruth Bell
1944	Hosts radio program called *Songs in the Night* in Chicago
1944	First attempt at mass evangelism at the inaugural rally for Chicagoland Youth for Christ
1944	Begins to preach regularly at Youth for Christ rallies
September 1945	Ruth Graham gives birth to their first child, Virginia Leftwich (Gigi)
1947	Becomes president of Northwestern Schools, Minneapolis, Minnesota
May 1948	Second child, Anne, is born

1949	Revival in Los Angeles brings Graham national attention
1950	Boston revival draws immense crowd on Boston Common
1950	Organizes Billy Graham Evangelistic Association (BGEA)
1950	Begins radio program *Hour of Decision*
December 1950	Daughter Ruth Bell (Bunny) is born
1950	President Harry Truman invites Billy to the White House
1952	Resigns as president of Northwestern Schools
1952	Washington, D.C., crusade includes a service at U.S. Capitol
July 1952	Son William Franklin Graham III is born
1952	Spends Christmas week on Korean war front
1953	Publishes first book, *Peace with God*
1953	At Chattanooga revival Graham allows mixed seating of whites and blacks
1954	London crusade at Harringay Arena; meets Winston Churchill
1956	Tours India
1957	New York crusade at Madison Square Garden
May 1958	Son Nelson Edman (Ned) Graham is born
1959	Crusades in Australia and New Zealand
1960	Assists Richard Nixon in losing campaign against John F. Kennedy
1962	Chicago rally at Soldier Field draws huge crowd
1962–63	Visits a number of Latin American countries, including Columbia, Brazil, and Argentina
1963	Meets with President Lyndon Johnson five days after Kennedy's assassination
1965	Graham's film company, World-Wide Pictures, releases *The Restless Ones*
1966	Meets with troops in Vietnam
1967	Visits Yugoslavia, Graham's first preaching in communist country
1968	Becomes insider in Richard Nixon's successful run for president
1969	Richard Nixon elected president with Graham's support

1970	Vietnam War protesters heckle Nixon and Graham in Knoxville
1972	Explo 72 in Dallas, a mass religious training and music festival, brings together Jesus Movement; Graham gives keynote address
1973	Billy and Ruth open crusade in South Korea
1974	Assembles 2,400 Protestant leaders from 150 countries at Lausanne, Switzerland
1975	Crusades in China
1977	Visits Hungary
1978	Crusade in Poland
1982	Preaches in Moscow at height of Cold War
1983	Receives Presidential Medal of Freedom from President Ronald Reagan
1983	More than 4,000 delegates meet in Holland for "Amsterdam '83"
1984	Crusade in Russia
1986	"Amsterdam '86" draws 10,000 itinerant evangelists
1992	Meets with President Kim Il Sung of North Korea
1995	Global Mission telecast in 117 languages in 185 countries from Puerto Rico
March 1995	Graham crusade in Puerto Rico received by satellite in 165 countries
1996	President Bill Clinton presents Billy and Ruth with the Congressional Gold Medal
2000	Graham retires as head of BGEA; Franklin Graham appointed chief executive officer
June 2000	Billy Graham Louisville crusade
September 14, 2001	Delivers message at Washington National Cathedral on National Day of Prayer and Remembrance following September 11 tragedy
June 2002	Leads crusade in Cincinnati, Ohio
May 2003	Leads four-day preaching mission in San Diego, breaking attendance records in Qualcomm Stadium

Chapter 1

FROM TAMPA TO NEW YORK

Twenty-five pairs of Baptist eyes measured the young man standing before a congregation in a small church in north Florida. On Easter Sunday evening, 1937, a gangling, blond, teenage student from the Florida Bible Institute prepared to preach a sermon. Never had he done this before.

Young Billy Graham had accompanied the academic dean of the Institute, the Reverend John Minder, and his family on a short vacation. Minder's friend, the Reverend Cecil Underwood, a part-time preacher and painter in the little town of Bostwick, greeted Minder with an expected invitation to preach the sermon that evening at his small church. Minder deferred, announcing to the surprise of both Underwood and Billy himself that the young student would preach that evening.

Although surprised by the turn of events, Billy was not totally unprepared for this moment. Throughout his childhood he had recited Bible passages and prayed aloud before his family and at church. At revivals and at the Institute, he had heard some of the celebrated evangelists of the day, from Billy Sunday to Mordecai Ham. He had seen them mesmerize their audiences with fiery admonitions to follow the Bible's commands and obey God's law or suffer the eternal consequences. He had watched their mannerisms, how they raised and lowered their voices to effect, how they moved rhythmically, and how they swept their listeners up in a frenzy of both fright and the promise of everlasting life.

Now, in front of those people in the pews, his mind seemed to go numb. All those passages that he had committed to memory raced through his mind; all his intentions to speak clearly and to pace himself vanished; all the images of the power and perfection of the preachers he wished to emulate were suddenly swept away in nervousness and anxiety. It was not that he forgot the words; it was that he remembered them all at once. Suddenly those words burst out of him like buckshot. He spoke so fast that many in the congregation were startled, puzzled over what they had just heard—or not heard. He thought that his failure had been total.

Instead, that night was the beginning.

Madison Square Garden, New York City. May 15, 1957—almost exactly 20 years after Graham first preached before an audience. At the site of some of the most memorable prizefights of the twentieth century the crowd rocks with anticipation, jostling to get a view of the main attraction: a man in the prime of his career, ready to take on his greatest challenge. He is not a prizefighter; he is an evangelist. This, however, is the Garden and it is ready for action.

He calls it the most important crusade of his life, a revival several weeks long that promises to dwarf in importance and impact any other he has ever undertaken. So infatuated with Graham's personality and presence has the nation become that President Dwight D. Eisenhower asked him to stop by the White House for a visit before his trip to New York. They talked about the need for a spiritual awakening throughout the land, one that would begin with a great religious crusade in New York.

The preacher's organization had prepared mightily. With a budget of nearly $1 million, it had ready a team of 2,000 ushers and 4,000 counselors to work with those in the audience who professed their desire to convert to Jesus Christ. It had involved numerous civic and religious groups to spread the word and arrange for transportation. There were the billboards, the car stickers, and the massive promotion on radio and television. The evening before the beginning of the crusade 10 churches hosted prayer vigils. The organizers emphasized at every turn that the crusade was open to all—Protestants, Catholics, Jews, and atheists. In the coming days, 8,000 prayer groups across the nation, plus 1,845 in 52 foreign countries, were poised to pray daily for the New York crusade's success.

Now the choir, a huge assemblage 1,500 strong, leads off with an old favorite:

Blessed assurance, Jesus is mine!
    O what a foretaste of glory divine!

From the floor of the Garden to the seats in the farthest rows, the audience stands and joins the chorus, a pulsating sound of joyous singing.

This is my story, this is my song,
Praising my Savior all the day long

Following the invocation are more songs, some scripture reading, announcements, and prayers. Now, from the side of the stage, the evangelist strides toward the pulpit. He is a tall and angular man with Nordic features; a shock of thick, wavy blond hair; prominent hands with long fingers; and penetrating blue eyes. He is silver screen material, a striking figure over whom movie casting agents would have fought pitched battles; but his agent, he believes, is the Lord. That's why he's in the Garden this night.

The evangelist had misgivings about New York. The city's writers and newspaper reporters were notorious for destroying all manner of speakers, idealists, and promoters who dared to tell the residents of the metropolis how to live their lives. "I seriously doubt that New York can be reached," Graham said in a candid observation. "If I knew what I had to go through there I would probably flee with terror. But if the city can be reached, God will do it. . . . If a few people are won to Christ, we'll be extremely happy. Our object is to win people to Christ. Secondarily, we hope the whole city will become God-conscious, that religion will be a talking point in the bars, in the subways, in the barbershops." He even used a metaphor most sacred in the Christian religion. "I'm prepared to go to New York," he said, "to be crucified if necessary."[1]

If the evangelist himself had doubts about a Christian evangelistic crusade in New York City—in Madison Square Garden no less—he had detractors and enemies aplenty.

Members of numerous religious persuasions—from Jews to Catholics—were repulsed by the evangelist's Bible-beating fundamentalist revivalism. Others were uninterested, amused, or hostile. Even certain ministers, worshippers, and theologians who accepted the message of the evangelist did not support the methods employed in religious revivals and had little confidence in the results.

Now, as he steps forward to deliver the message this night, Graham is prepared both physically and mentally. For weeks, he spent full days in his native North Carolina woods running and hiking and honing his sermon delivery. In preparing for the Garden, he told a reporter that he has to train like a prizefighter. Once a crusade begins, from three o'clock in the afternoon until the meeting time, he has to be alone. Even his wife doesn't disturb him. He exercises, practices lines, and tries to nap. He worries that if he doesn't pace himself, he will be exhausted and ineffective at the end of the crusade. On this night, however, the 39-year-old battler for the Lord is in perfect shape, "hard as rock," says one of his workers.

The mammoth crowd gradually quiets as Billy Graham steps forward. "About three years ago," he says, "we were approached about the possibility of coming to New York City. We were frightened at the prospect. And tonight I think we are more fearful than even then, as we contemplate the responsibility and the overwhelming opportunity that God has given to the churches of New York in the next few weeks."[2]

Graham addresses the myths about the upcoming crusade. Some people, he says, believe it is an effort to clean up the social and political ills of New York; others that it is an effort to promote Republican politicians; and still others that it is a massive promotion to create more Baptists. It is none of these, he says.

"We have come to New York," Billy declares, "with the express purpose of winning men and women to a saving knowledge of Jesus Christ." Judging by his solemn manner and the tone of his voice, almost everyone who heard him that night knew that he was serious.

NOTES

1. *New York Mirror*, 11 May 1957.
2. *New York Times*, 16 May 1957.

Chapter 2

A FARM BOY
BECOMES A PREACHER

From his earliest days, Billy Graham's family and acquaintances called him Billy Frank. He was born on November 7, 1918, in the downstairs bedroom of a farmhouse near Charlotte, North Carolina, the first of four children born to Morrow Coffey Graham and her husband, William "Frank" Graham, a dairy farmer.

This was a time of milk in glass bottles in which cream rose to the top, a time when local dairies delivered to the homes of customers. Frank Graham, who had only three years of formal education, had acquired through solid determination and hard work about 75 cows and 400 regular customers. Red barns flanked the white frame house with green trim; tenant farmers helped with the work.

The family's roots were deeply Southern. Both of Billy Graham's grandfathers, William Crook Graham, Frank Graham's father, and Ben Coffey, Morrow's father, had fought for the Confederacy in the Civil War. A veteran of the Sixth South Carolina Volunteers, William Crook Graham carried in his leg a ball fired from a Union gun. Coffey, of the Eleventh North Carolina Regiment, had lost a leg and an eye at Gettysburg.

A large man with dark wavy hair, Frank Graham had such a strong work ethic that friends and family doubted whether he had ever participated in any sport or game other than card playing, or if he even went fishing. He did puff on an occasional cigar. When Crook Graham died in 1910, Frank Graham was just 20 years old and had assumed the responsibility for turning around a run-down farm. With much hard work and with the help of his brother, Clyde, and other relatives he succeeded. He did so with good humor—despite the rigors of life on the farm, Frank would entertain his neighbors by spinning tales and telling jokes.

Morrow Graham had been raised on a small vegetable farm near Charlotte. Slight in frame with long blond hair, she seemed delicate—an appearance that belied much grit and feistiness. Morrow spent a year at Elizabeth College, where instructors taught young girls proper dress, manners, and music. Early on, she took seriously her worship in a local Presbyterian church.

Frank Graham and Morrow Coffey courted for six years before marrying. Frank had wanted to be absolutely certain of his financial security before entering into marriage. When they finally married, Frank and Morrow did it in style, honeymooning in Asheville, North Carolina, at the exclusive Biltmore House.

Morrow, who had more schooling than Frank, took over the records and billing of the dairy farm. Never slowing down, Frank was up at the earliest hours, constantly improvising ways to improve the business, hiring new tenant farmers to work the pastures, bringing in water and electricity, and turning a modest dairy enterprise into one of the most thriving in the area.

Billy Graham was born two years after the marriage of Frank and Morrow. He was so hyperactive as a child that his mother once took him to a local doctor, fearful that something was wrong. The diagnosis: an unusually high level of energy.

The Graham household would soon add new members. Catherine Graham was born two years after Billy, and then Melvin Graham, Billy's brother. It would be another eight years before another sister, Jean, arrived.

Racing at full tilt through his childhood, young Graham, tall and thin with a shock of blond hair, helped milk the cows, devoured Tarzan and Robin Hood books, played practical jokes, chased goats, romped with dogs, occasionally hunted and fished, and dreamed of becoming a baseball player. Along with his sisters and brother, he learned to ride mules bareback. During rainstorms, he loved to sneak off to one of the hay barns, climb up in the rafters, and listen to raindrops hit the tin roof. He said later that those times alone in the hayloft, with solitude and time to think, helped shape his character.

Graham would later remember these early years with much respect, love, and admiration for his parents. Although they quarreled occasionally, Billy never heard a word of profanity from either of them. He developed close ties with all his siblings, but especially with Melvin. They shared a room with twin beds and, together, took on increasing work responsibilities. Graham recalled that the advantage of physical strength he enjoyed over his younger brother gave way in their teenage years to Melvin's muscular frame.

Graham's Scottish-Presbyterian parents provided the boy with a strict moral code that stood in opposition to the so-called Roaring Twenties, a time of illegal booze and fast dancing. The family prayed daily together and attended the Associate Reformed Presbyterian Church in downtown Charlotte. Billy's mother insisted that he begin to memorize various passages in the Bible. Graham later recalled that when he was around 10 years old his family visited an aunt who asked the children to spend some time during their visit reading the Bible. Billy went to work on the task and then returned in about 10 minutes bragging that he had read one entire book of the holy word. He had indeed done just that—it was the Epistle of Jude, the shortest book in the New Testament. It is one page long.

Young Graham and his family took to heart the preacher's railings against the demons of smoking, drinking, lusting, and gambling. Graham's father had often told the family and anyone else who would listen of his religious conversion at an evangelistic crusade when he was a teenager. Frank Graham's dry sense of humor contrasted with his strict discipline of his children, sometimes enforced by spanking. "I learned to obey without questioning," Billy Graham later wrote. "Lying, cheating, stealing, and property destruction are foreign to me. I was taught that laziness was one of the worst evils."[1]

When Graham was six years old, his father took the boy to Charlotte to hear a traveling evangelist who had once been a center fielder for baseball's Chicago White Stockings. The evangelist's name was Billy Sunday and he drew a huge crowd. Wide-eyed, the young boy took it all in—the spectacle of thousands gathering in a tent to sing and pray and the scintillating sermon delivered by the athletic evangelist who pranced around the tabernacle platform like a circus performer.

The work on the farm was from before dawn to after dark. Due to his responsibilities as the oldest child, from milking cows and cleaning out stalls to acting as a delivery boy and hauling five-gallon silver milk cans, Graham's schoolwork suffered. Although he sometimes got only three or four hours of sleep a night, he did manage to attain average grades.

It was not until Graham was nine years old that the family was able to build a two-story brick Colonial house with indoor plumbing on the property. Bathing in a washtub on the back porch was at last a thing of the past.

Only occasionally did the family venture beyond the confines of the farm to attend community events and movies or to visit the ocean (especially Myrtle Beach, South Carolina) for a few days in summer. The first long trip Billy made with his family was to Washington, D.C. They did not stay long. After rushing around the Smithsonian Institution in 40 minutes, they climbed every one of the 896 steps of the Washington Monument.

It was a carefully controlled existence, one defined by the pressures and expectations of a strict and pietistic farm family living through the changing seasons of work, the reward of simple pleasures, and the natural cycles of birth and death.

Living in a rural setting did satisfy one particular craving for young Graham—wheels. By age eight he had steered a GMC truck and by the time he was 10 he had driven a Model-T Ford on the rough roads near the farm. He later admitted to strong tendencies toward showing off, once recklessly plowing into the heavy mud of a sinkhole with several friends aboard. It took a team of mules to pull the car out of the muck. He also admitted to having something of a lead foot on the accelerator.

Graham also had an early interest in girls. His sister Catherine later said with more than a hint of exaggeration that Billy seemed to have another girlfriend every day. Many of the teenage girls were definitely interested in him, with his fierce blue eyes, blond hair, ready smile, and access to a car.

At Sharon High School, on the edge of Charlotte, Billy managed only a C average. Although not inclined to troublemaking, he did get into a few fistfights. A couple of times, he remembered later, he was beaten up slightly.

In his first formal experience speaking from a prepared text, the young Graham was draped in a long Uncle Sam costume, a fake beard, and tall hat for a school play. When he got up to recite the lines, he perspired profusely and his knees shook. He vowed never to be a public speaker.

Although he had a passion for baseball, Graham played for the high school team only as a substitute. He could field but was a weak hitter. He held the bat in a cross-handed grip because it felt more natural. Unfortunately, very few successful baseball hitters have used such a grip.

In the fall of 1934, about the time of Graham's seventeenth birthday, the Reverend Mordecai Ham, a well-known revivalist preacher from Louisville, Kentucky, arrived in Charlotte to begin a three-month evangelistic campaign. Ham was an old-time Bible thumper whose sermons were not only a call to accept Christ as savior but also a challenge to his listeners to give up the moral evils and sinful behavior so prevalent in what he saw as a decaying, corrupt society. Bespectacled, neatly dressed, sporting a carefully trimmed mustache, Ham looked more like an accountant than a rescuer of souls. In spite of this, he rained down on the somewhat terrified gathering a withering assault on sin, even graphically describing a lake of fire that awaited sinners if they did not forsake their evil ways.

When the Ham revival opened in Charlotte, Graham had no desire to attend. A few weeks later, however, a group of friends decided to see what all the hoopla was about in the ramshackle pine tabernacle on the out-skirts of town. Graham was stunned by the scene—the music, the oratory, the calls for repentance, the gestures of townspeople who publicly de-clared their faith by marching down the sawdust rail to the platform. The scene was mesmerizing.

Captivated, Graham came to the services night after night. He met Grady Wilson and his brother Thomas Walter (T. W.), sons of a local plumber, and others who would become friends and associates for life.

Somehow, Graham felt as if Mordecai Ham, in his railings against sin and evil, was talking to him personally. It was as if the evangelist would, on many of those nights, point his bony hand right at Graham, demand-ing that the boy give up all sinfulness that might be lurking—drinking, carousing, all of the things that Graham had never done but that he might at some time do. Somehow, guilt and self-condemnation fell over this teenager whose thorniest moral deficiency had likely been reckless driv-ing. Graham later remembered ducking behind the broad-brimmed hat of a lady sitting in front of him, so sure was he that Ham was singling him out for moral weakness. Even so, Graham kept coming back to the tabernacle to hear the preacher again.

At the end of one of the services, the preacher issued the usual call for converts. Graham found himself marching down the aisle to give public notice that he was committing his life to the Lord. "When my decision for Christ was made," he said, "I walked slowly down and knelt in prayer. I opened my heart and knew for the first time the sweetness and joy of God, of truly being born again."[2] Mordecai Ham later said that before the Char-lotte Campaign, young Billy Graham's hero had been Babe Ruth; it was now Jesus Christ.

During his last year of high school, Graham, encouraged by his parents, made it a point to hear almost all of the traveling evangelists that came through Charlotte. One of the evangelists, Jimmie Johnson, took up Frank Graham's offer to stay at the farmhouse. On one weekend, Johnson took Billy to a small jail where the evangelist conducted a service. Unexpectedly, he asked Billy to say a few words about what it was like to be converted. The nervous teenager stood up and began to stammer through a brief testimony about how it was to be converted to the gospel of Jesus Christ. The prison-ers, Billy later recalled, looked off in different directions or picked their teeth. It was the first time Graham ever professed his faith in public.

During the Jimmie Johnson revival, Graham and several of his friends, including Grady and T. W., joined a Tuesday night Bible-study group led by the wife of a telephone company executive. Religion was now a central part of Graham's life. In the spring of 1936, Graham graduated with a class of 25 students from Sharon High School. In the yearbook he noted that his goal was to become a minister of the gospel.

The route to the ministry led through college. During Graham's senior year at Sharon, Bob Jones, head of Bob Jones College in Cleveland, Tennessee, and a dynamic fundamentalist speaker, made an appearance at the school. Graham's parents decided that Bob Jones College was the place for their aspiring student of the gospel. Jimmie Johnson had been a graduate of Bob Jones and both T. W. and Grady also decided to attend Jones. That was enough to convince Billy. He agreed to enroll.

The Graham family suffered financially during the Great Depression of the thirties. At one point, the family's savings were nearly depleted. Nevertheless, Frank and Morrow Graham agreed to pay for Billy's enrollment. Billy, however, felt he needed more pocket change than the family would provide. When a friend of the family offered young Graham a job as a salesman for the Fuller Brush Company, a national company that used door-to-door salesmen, he leaped at the chance. His route was not near Charlotte but in eastern South Carolina. For the first time in his life, Graham left the dairy farm to live apart from his parents, his brother Melvin, and his two sisters, Catherine and Jean.

Billy Graham took to sales like Brer Rabbit took to the brier patch—it was the place for him. All that indefatigable energy, that moxie and instinct for presenting the product, that aura of sincerity and purpose that crowds across the world would see in the future, were now being honed on Fuller Brush customers. He studied the catalogs to learn the facts about the brushes; he convinced himself that every house in his area of South Carolina needed more than one Fuller brush; he perfected his sales pitch and tailored his spiel to suit various individuals.

He defied setbacks. On one occasion, after he had rung a doorbell, a lady threw a bucket of water on his head from an upstairs window. He persevered. He learned to get his foot in the door and to close the sale before the door. He learned a great deal about communicating a message and connecting with a variety of people. Characteristically, he went about the job with more than twice the vigor of the average teenage Fuller Brush salesman.

In September 1936, his father drove Graham, Grady, and T. W. across the Appalachian Mountains into east Tennessee to enroll in Bob Jones College. From his first days at the school, Graham felt entirely uncomfortable. The boy who had raced around backcountry roads in a Model-T was now corralled. A prison could not have drawn up a more restrictive code of behavior. For example, a couple on a date could not hold hands or sit on the same sofa. The school monitored the mail to ensure purity. Graham also disliked the authoritarian teaching methods of the school that left little or no room for intellectual discourse or debate. By Christmas vacation, Graham was chafing at the prospect of continuing at the college.

When the family visited Florida on a short vacation over the holidays, Graham and his parents became interested in the Florida Bible Institute, a school near Tampa. In late January Graham transferred, but not until a final valedictory meeting with Dr. Bob Jones. Graham remembers the dire warning directed his way. "If you leave here," Dr. Bob warned the teenager, "...the chances are you'll never be heard of. At best, all you could amount to would be a poor country Baptist preacher somewhere out in the sticks."[3]

Graham found in the Institute everything he had not found at Bob Jones, from its setting in Florida's sunshine to its less confining social atmosphere to its individual instruction. Here he found a refreshing blend of religion and philosophy and differing viewpoints that crossed denominational boundaries. Here, he found teachers who became lifelong friends. They frequently took groups of students to other towns, visiting churches, jails, and missions, all in an effort to provide a real world grounding in what it meant to give personal Christian witness.

Dean John Minder, a dean of the Institute and pastor of the Tampa Gospel Tabernacle, took a personal interest in the progress of this rail-thin farm boy; it was he who encouraged Graham to preach his first sermon on Easter Sunday, 1937, at Bostwick Baptist Church in Palatka, Florida.

It was at the Institute that Graham also saw some of the well known Christian evangelical leaders who were invited to speak—from the evangelist Gipsy Smith, by that time an aging gospel warrior, to Homer Rodeheaver, Billy Sunday's musical director who had founded his own Christian training organization, to big-time radio preacher Gerald Winrod. He took notes at their lectures and studied their mannerisms. He even caddied for some of those who golfed and had his picture taken with them. Despite his awkward early attempts at public speaking, Graham's experiences with the preachers convinced him that his religious instruction was leading to his own calling as a preacher.

In March 1938, Graham later remembered, he was returning from a walk across the eighteenth green of a nearby golf course. With no golfers heading down the fairway, he decided to sit down on the green. It was there, he said, that he made his decision to become a preacher. "Oh God," he remembered praying, "If you want me to preach, I will do it."[4]

He began to memorize and practice sermons from outlines he had learned in school. Frequently, he paddled a canoe to a little island close to the Institute where he tried out his oratory on an audience of birds, alligators, and other creatures. Occasionally, folks riding boats near the island could hear the exuberant, if clumsy, evangelical harangues rising and falling in intensity. His friends often teased him about possible converts among the fauna. Graham, however, was now channeling his enormous energy and drive. Now, he told himself, he would push himself with everything he could muster to make himself a preacher worthy of his promise to the Lord.

If Graham's attentions were riveted on matters theological and plans to become a preacher, they were also riveted on a girl named Emily Cavanaugh. Attractive and bright, with dark hair and eyes that Billy thought sparkled, Emily so entranced the young Graham that, at age 18, he asked her to marry him—in writing. Billy had spent time with Emily at the Cavanaughs' house on Sunday nights before a church youth group and, as he said later, he had fallen hard. She had accompanied him on some of his preaching assignments, riding in his 1929 Chevrolet coupe.

The attraction was mutual. Emily said yes to Billy's proposal after they had attended a service at a black church. Graham's fiancée, however, changed her mind after several months and broke off the engagement. She told Billy that she had fallen for a mutual friend, another fledgling preacher named Charles Massey. Friends of the two later revealed that Emily wanted to marry someone who would probably amount to something and that Billy did not seem a likely success, while Charles did.

Devastated, Graham, with an intensity that a teenager's first love can engender, wrote to a friend that the stars had fallen from the sky and that life was barely worth living. He said it was like Paradise Lost. He retreated into a solemnity that he had never before experienced.

As he saw himself failing in romance, Graham determined that he would not fail at preaching. He began to hold outdoor services with a gospel quartet or a soloist everywhere he could draw a crowd. He ventured out to a dog racetrack and preached in the parking lot. He stood on boxes on street corners, often attracting scores of hecklers and their derisive laughter. He spoke at a mission to Hispanic teenagers, using a translator, and at trailer parks; at one of them, the Tin Can Trailer Park, he often drew crowds of several hundred. He once tried to preach about the sins of alcohol in front of a bar in Tampa's tenderloin area only to have the saloonkeeper grab the young orator, shove his face in some mud in front of the bar, and tell him never to come back.

Graham was undeterred, frenetically bounding around the Tampa area like a man possessed, ascending the platform at rescue missions, accepting occasional requests to fill in at small churches. In Tampa, there is now a historical marker at a street corner where Graham used to speak as many as seven times a day on Sundays.

In the summer of 1938, Graham opened a small revival near the church where he had preached his first sermon in Palatka, Florida. The revival was held at the East Palatka Baptist Church and sponsored by a nearby youth group who had become aware of Billy's preaching through the Reverend Cecil Underwood, in whose church Billy had preached that first sermon. Graham stayed with the Underwood family, helping with chores during the day and preaching at the church at night. All of Billy's practice before the birds and alligators on the island, all the efforts on street corners and in missions and in trailer parks had led to this time—a revival of his own.

Although the revival was modest and had small audiences, it was very well received. A local newspaper said that Graham was sensational, an orator who did not mince words, who told the crowd that they were headed for the same hell as the criminal and the bootlegger if they did not give up the things of the world that were ugly in God's sight.

Graham was also invited by local radio station WFOY in nearby St. Augustine to make appearances. All of this together—the street speaking, the short revival, the radio messages—gave Graham increasing confidence that he could succeed in the business marked out by those evangelists he had seen at the Institute, whose words he had so assiduously written down, and whose platform presence and gestures he had carefully studied.

The East Palatka revival also marked another milestone in the life of Graham—he became a Baptist. If Billy were to lead a revival at the Baptist Church, Reverend Underwood suggested, it might be proper to be officially part of the Baptist faith. It was not a hard decision for Graham, who was never caught up in the denominational differences of the Christian faith. If a person believed in Christ as the savior and if that person was born again and dedicated his or her life to Christianity, it made little difference to Graham what denominational ties he or she had.

Baptists believe that a saved person should be baptized by immersion soon after being born again, so Billy soon found himself, along with some other converts, out at nearby Silver Lake wading into the water where Reverend Underwood lowered him under and lifted him out. He had shed his Presbyterian roots and, for the rest of his life, would refer to himself as a Baptist. Several months after his baptism, he was formally ordained as an evangelist by the St. John's Baptist Association of Northern Florida.

In the spring of 1940, the Florida Bible Institute held commencement services. Billy Graham, age 21, was the overwhelming choice of his 10 fellow classmates as "soul winner" and president of the class.

By the time he finished his studies at the Florida Bible Institute, Graham had put together the core of sermons with which he would begin his career. They were heavily infused with calls to forsake the wretched sins plaguing humanity—from demon rum to crime to motion pictures, many of which he regarded as immoral. The sermons were also patriotic, calling attention to the sinfulness and immoral political philosophies dominating much of the world outside the boundaries of the United States. He saw natural disasters as a sign of God's wrath, calling for people to repent and accept the truths of the Bible or face the consequences. None of this material was new. It was standard fundamentalist fare. In the hands of a dedicated young evangelist who firmly believed that God had called him to bear witness to the world, however, the material was all he would need to make an impact.

NOTES

1. Graham, *Just As I Am*, p. 22.
2. Busby, *God's Ambassador*, p. 33.
3. Martin, *Prophet with Honor*, p. 70.
4. Busby, *God's Ambassador*, p. 35.

Chapter 3

WHEATON AND RUTH

Over a hundred years before Billy Graham graduated from the Florida Bible Institute, a man named Warren Wheaton, age 25, arrived in Chicago, Illinois, from Connecticut. He had come by railroad and then by steamboat. He soon laid claim to 640 acres of land west of the city. His brother, Jesse, an apprenticed carpenter, spent several months working in Chicago before joining him. Jesse later claimed 300 acres of land adjoining his brother's property. In 1848, the Wheaton brothers and a friend, Erastus Gary, gave the railroad three miles of right-of-way and the grateful railroad officials named the depot Wheaton. In 1850, the Wheaton brothers began to encourage others to build a community around the railroad station. Soon, lots had been surveyed and the formal plan of the town of Wheaton was filed with the county.

When Warren Wheaton befriended Jonathan Blanchard, an educator, social activist, and fellow pioneer, they shared a common vision for the town—it would be home to a community and an educational institution emphasizing religion and church-related education. Warren donated land for the development of a Christian liberal arts institution, later called Wheaton College. On January 9, 1860, the college welcomed its first classes. It would become a stronghold for Fundamentalist Christian education.

The town of Wheaton and its college would become extremely important to Billy Graham. It would give him additional education and a wife.

It the fall of 1940, with the European war taking a terrible toll abroad and with the prospects of United States intervention increasing, Billy Graham, 21 years old, a graduate of the Florida Bible Institute and ordained Baptist minister, arrived at Wheaton. Due to the Florida Bible Institute's lack of accreditation standards, few of his courses were acceptable to Wheaton, so Graham had nearly a full college career ahead of him.

It was through members of the family of Dr. V. Raymond Edman, the new president of Wheaton, that Billy entered the college. Elner Edman, brother of the college president, had heard Graham preach at the Tampa Gospel Tabernacle. He and others of the family praised Graham as a possible future Christian leader, and encouraged V. Raymond Edman to recommend his entrance to Wheaton. When Graham admitted that neither he nor his family had the money to pay for a Wheaton education, Elner Edman and a friend agreed to pay for his first year and to use their influence to try to get him a scholarship for the remaining years.

Billy was jubilant. Dr. Edman, a former professor of political science, was the college's fourth president and had replaced long-time president J. Oliver Buswell. Apparently, years earlier, Graham's mother was once so entranced by a Buswell sermon that she prayed that her son would someday attend Wheaton College. It was not surprising that Graham had become a student at Wheaton, his mother would later remark. After all, he had been prayed into the place. It would be Edman, not Buswell, who would guide the college's course through the World War II years and through the student life of Billy Graham.

Boyish and lean with a square jaw and strong nose and a crop of wavy blond hair, young Billy Graham seemed to everyone a true concoction of decency. Polite, seemingly naive, and forever earnest, he mixed with the Illinois students like a foreigner. His language was different, his slow cadence contrasting with the way his boundless energy carried him breathlessly around campus. He later said that when he first walked among the stately buildings and manicured campus grounds, he felt like a hick. He was older than many of the students, and with his background of street-corner oratory, he seemed to some almost a seasoned veteran. Many of them called him "Preacher."

Ruth Bell was also a student at Wheaton when Billy arrived for fall classes in 1940. Ruth was born in China and spent her young years in both China and Korea. She was the daughter of a distinguished Presbyterian missionary surgeon, Dr. L. Nelson Bell, head of the Tsingkiang General Hospital. The hospital had been founded in 1887 by the father of Pearl Buck, the internationally renowned writer and advocate of human rights.

It was common among missionaries to send their children back to the United States to attend college. The Bells had chosen a school with a reputation for both biblical fundamentalism and academic excellence. To her friends at Wheaton, it seemed as if Ruth had already planned her life and would not be distracted. She had a vision, she said, of devoting herself to God as a missionary to nomadic Tibetan tribes in the Himalayas. She would not marry. She would use her college career to gain knowledge of the Tibetan language and to intensify her study of the Bible.

For most young college students, such goals would have seemed visionary if not peculiar. Ruth, however, had seen many things that other students, including Billy Graham, had only read about in books. Much of what she had seen had been intensely disturbing. Along with her sister, Rosa, she had witnessed the tragedy of war and the crucible of plague and pestilence; she had experienced the political and military turmoil surrounding the Nationalist Chinese government, the opposition Communist insurgents, and Japanese invaders. She had seen the bodies of infants lying alongside roads. She had seen displaced people wandering in the streets, homeless and desperate. She had heard gunfire and artillery from nearby skirmishes and seen the injured and dead. She had seen people foraging for the little amount of food sometimes available. She had avoided packs of rats thriving in the unsanitary conditions.

In the midst of the turmoil, she had developed a particular need to rescue animals and birds suffering in the throes of war. She cared for their wounds and saved them from starvation. At a young age, under the influence of her extremely religious parents, she had developed, despite the poverty and cruelty around her, a strong belief in God. She prayed intensely, kept a personal journal, and began to write poetry.

She gained increasing respect for the talented and deeply motivated people around whom she grew up—the missionaries and their families. She often pointed out that theirs was something of a frontier existence, with limited contact with the outside world, a minimum of provisions, and the fear of bandits on the loose. The missionaries laughed, radiated joy, and worked exceedingly hard at what they did. They shared a cause and discovered meaning for their lives in it.

In 1934, Ruth was sent from China to a prestigious Christian institution in northern Korea, the Pyongyang Foreign School. It was known as one of the finest schools in Asia, drawing students from around the world. To Ruth, however, it was like exile, separating her from the surroundings she had known, from her parents, and from the sense of security, however scant, she had been able to develop in her life. She later said that she nearly died of homesickness in Korea, even though her sister was already at the school. Her journal entries from the period are filled with sadness and yearning for stability.

In her spartan dormitory room, she felt overwhelming homesickness, crying herself to sleep night after night. She was later able to look back at this period as her training period, her "boot camp." She would see the experience in Pyongyang as a positive, life-altering trial and would be grateful for it. Despite the hardships, or because of them, she developed a keen sense of self-assuredness and boldness.

It was Graham's friend Johnny Streater who first told Billy about this extraordinary individual who had spent all of her life overseas. Streater owned a pickup truck and paid Billy 50 cents an hour to haul furniture and luggage for local residents as well as students. Streater and his fiancée were studying Chinese and planned to go to China as missionaries after graduation. Ruth Bell had not only become a valuable friend to both of them but had also been able to share invaluable first-hand recollections. Many of the students at Wheaton shared stories about Ruth's experiences abroad. They admired her courage and religious piety.

Johnny Streater became an eager matchmaker, and, as he and Billy made their rounds in the truck, he often suggested that Graham and Ruth get together for a date. Streater talked about her world experiences, her religious bent, and her vivaciousness. He told Billy that Ruth had already rejected several would-be suitors but that Billy might be different. The opportunity came one day in November 1940 when Graham and Streater left the library to go to lunch and ran across Ruth in the hallway, chatting with friends. Streater introduced them. Graham later said that although he politely went through the formalities, he had experienced a sudden rush of excitement.

Ruth had already noticed Billy on campus. "I first saw him running down the steps as I was going up. I thought to myself, 'There is a young man in a hurry.' As I got to know him, I was so impressed with his commitment to the Lord."[1]

At student prayer time, with the men on one side of a hallway and the women on the other, Ruth became increasingly impressed with Graham's forthrightness, his ability to pray aloud, and his commitment to his religion. "I remember telling the Lord, 'If you let me spend my life with that man, it would be the greatest privilege I could think of.'"[2]

Graham invited Ruth to accompany him to the school's presentation of Handel's *Messiah*. She accepted. Soon, Graham's attentions were focused on Ruth and little else. Seeing Graham's mounting preoccupation with Ruth, Streater, the matchmaker who had brought the two together, now expressed concern to Billy that perhaps everything was moving rather too quickly, that Billy was rushing madly into something that he might not want.

Graham heeded his warning. For a time, he began to stay away from Ruth as much as he could. When they passed each other on campus, Billy tried to seem indifferent. It was a strategy that both disturbed and confused her. Nevertheless, when Ruth sent him a note in early February inviting him to a party, Graham accepted and in turn asked her to attend church with him on a Friday night when he was scheduled to preach. She also accepted. Later, after the church service, she jotted down in her journal that Billy demonstrated in his preaching a remarkable quality of humility and fearlessness.

Billy wrote to his mother that he had found the woman he would one day marry. He loved Ruth, he told his mother, because Ruth looked just like her. His mother destroyed the letter, not only somewhat embarrassed by the remark but also fearing that Ruth might some day discover it and be insulted.

Despite his deep attraction to Ruth, Graham exhibited some of the authoritarian tendencies that had prevailed at the Graham household. He badgered Ruth about personal habits, suggesting over and over again certain foods she should eat and that she should get more exercise. At one point, he needled Ruth about the woman's place in a relationship, saying she should search the Scriptures and pray until the path God intended had become clear and for her to let him know when she had decided to accept that place. After all, in the world of the rural North Carolina farm, a woman was there to be the gentle but submissive and largely invisible force in the family. After all, his own mother did not even own a driver's license because her husband didn't think women should drive cars. At the same time, Graham knew that it was his mother who kept the books for the farm and ran the house.

In April 1941, Billy and Ruth had their most serious quarrel, and it revolved around this significant issue. Ruth wrote to her mother that sometimes Graham was not easy to love because of his dogmatic and unwavering opinions. She still suspected that the mountains of the Himalayas might be in her future, rather than a life with Billy Graham.

If Billy was subconsciously attempting to force his potential wife into the mold of his mother, Ruth was having none of it. To Ruth, Graham's view of a woman in a relationship as a submissive and silent partner was galling. If Ruth's religious views were mostly orthodox, her spirit and growing confidence in her own abilities were not. Even when Graham threatened to end the relationship during a quarrel, Ruth stood her ground on the issue. It was Graham who backed off his rigid stands.

In the spring of 1941, just before leaving campus for the summer, he asked her to marry him. He later remembered thinking that he had become so infatuated with Ruth that he would have been tempted to consider spending his life in the mountains of Tibet, of which she had dreamed, if that was the only way he could be with her.

While in Florida delivering sermons in Dr. John Minder's church, he finally got his answer. In a letter postmarked July 6, 1941, she wrote, "I'll
marry you." After delivering his sermon that night, Billy recalled, he
could not remember anything he had said. On July 7, she wrote to her parents, "To be with Bill in work won't be easy. There will be little financial
backing, lots of obstacles and criticism, and no earthly glory whatsoever."[3]
Still, she would not experience peace, she said, unless she made this decision, one she knew was consistent with the Lord's wishes.

In the summer of 1941, Graham met Ruth's parents, who had been
forced to leave China because of the Japanese invasion. There had been
fighting between the Japanese and Chinese for years, but all-out war had
broken out in 1937 and, as it progressively worsened, the Bells left China
and returned to the United States. They settled in Montreat, North Carolina, at the foot of Graybeard Mountain. It was a rustic community
founded many decades earlier as a spiritual retreat by Christian religious
leaders of several denominations for the encouragement of Christian work
and living. Billy showed up at the Bells' new Montreat home carrying an
engagement ring that he had purchased with most of the proceeds from a
series of sermons in Charlotte. He paid slightly over a hundred dollars for
the ring. It had a diamond, he said, so big that you could almost see it with
a magnifying glass. Ruth accepted it eagerly.

Just before she was to return to school in Illinois in 1941, Ruth, along
with her sister Rosa, became exceptionally ill. Her parents, suspecting
malaria, sent them both to a Presbyterian sanitarium in New Mexico, an
environment whose arid desert climate was considered helpful for various
pulmonary illnesses.

As she and her sister recovered, Ruth's thoughts again turned to missionary work and she began to question again her decision to marry Graham. With the doubts about her future life's work still troubling her deeply,
she wrote to him saying that it might be best to break off the engagement.
When she returned to school in January 1942, he offered to take the ring
back but asked her whether she thought the Lord had brought the two of
them together. After much soul searching, she had the answer. Yes, she believed, the Lord had indeed brought them together. She kept the ring.

After Japanese warplanes bombed Pearl Harbor in December 1941 and
the United States officially entered World War II, Graham offered his services as an army chaplain. He was told he needed to finish college and
complete a full year as a pastor to qualify. Graham worked to fulfill that re-
quirement.

After Billy and Ruth graduated from Wheaton College in June 1943,
Graham was invited to give a sermon at a tiny, half-built church in Western

Springs, Illinois, twenty miles from Chicago. The Village Baptist Church was, at the time, a basement with a temporary roof over it. So small was the congregation—only a few dozen members—that they had not yet been able to raise the funds to complete the building. When the few church members, jammed into the covered basement, first heard Billy Graham, they were startled—that rapid voice rising to decibels unfit for the space they occupied. At the same time, they were inspired. They offered the college-student preacher a salary of 45 dollars a week, and he accepted.

On Friday, August 13, 1943, 24-year-old Billy Graham married Ruth Bell in Montreat at the Presbyterian conference center. The service was conducted by Billy's mentor, John Minder. Dr. Kerr Taylor, a close friend of the Bells and fellow missionary, assisted in the service, along with a soloist from Chinkiang, China. After a short honeymoon in the resort town of Blowing Rock, North Carolina, they headed back to Western Springs. They took hikes, enjoyed the nearby arboretum, and occasionally went to the golf course, Billy as a player and Ruth as his caddy.

With his work as a pastor at Western Springs, Graham had fulfilled the requirements for his chaplainry in the army and was commissioned a second lieutenant. As the entrance time approached, however, Graham suffered a severe case of mumps, a disease that could be life threatening. He suffered for over six weeks with high temperatures and periods in which he became delirious. The already skinny Graham lost additional weight. Ruth feared for his life. One radio listener became so concerned for Graham's health that he sent a check for $100 and suggested that the preacher and his wife take a short trip to Florida. The couple accepted the offer. By the time Graham recovered, the war's end was near and the army's chief of chaplains granted him a discharge.

In January 1944, Graham, now 26, decided to take yet another step in his evangelical ministry—he turned to radio. When a Chicago-area pastor, Torrey Johnson, asked Graham to take over a weekly radio program called *Songs in the Night* on Chicago station WCFL, Billy eagerly accepted. Not only did he convince members of his congregation to contribute funds to launch his own version of the show; he managed to convince them that the church itself, or at least what had been built, was the place to host it. Every Sunday night, in this basement sanctuary, *Songs in the Night* reached out across the Chicago area with the fresh sounds of a dynamic preacher.

Graham immediately saw the potential of the program and he turned to a 37-year-old Christian soloist named George Beverly Shea to add an extra dimension. Shea was a veteran radio announcer at the Moody Bible Institute, an evangelical college in Chicago that had its own radio programming. He was also a regular on ABC's radio show *Clubtime* and the writer of a number of hymns including the well known "I'd Rather Have Jesus." "One morning in 1943 there was a rap at my office door," Shea remembered. "I opened it, and there stood a tall gentleman with a big smile waiting to say hello. I realized that I was meeting someone quite unusual."[4]

With the news that Graham was starting a radio program, his parents were somewhat concerned that Billy was taking on more than he could handle, despite his astonishing energy. He threw himself into the job of pastor at the same pace at which he threw himself into everything—frantic. He visited all the members of the Western Springs congregation at short intervals, encouraging them to bring their friends to the church. He launched a Western Suburban Professional Men's Club, persuading business executives with tight schedules but important connections to meet over dinners. He managed to draw crowds of more than 300 at a time to hear his speeches. Now he was taking on the duties of a radio minister. Morrow Graham wondered if even her son could keep up the schedule.

In spite of the Grahams' doubts, it was a remarkable road that their son was now on and they radiated pride. "We couldn't get the program on our house radio," Morrow said, "Mr. Graham and I sat in the car and tuned the radio dial until the station came in loud and clear. Then we sat back marveling and we'd say to each other, 'Imagine, that's our Billy Frank.' "[5]

NOTES

1. Dailey, "Conversation with Ruth Bell Graham."
2. "Uplifted by Faith," p. 155.
3. Martin, *Prophet with Honor*, p. 83.
4. Dailey, "Conversation with George Beverly Shea."
5. Busby, *God's Ambassador*, p. 39.

Chapter 4

ON THE ROAD
TO LOS ANGELES

YOUTH FOR CHRIST

"Geared to the Times, Anchored to the Rock," was its motto. It was Youth for Christ, a national evangelistic movement established especially for young people and returning servicemen. Its look was zoot suit, flashy, and young. Its tempo was upbeat, exuberant, with energy to spare. Its purpose was to celebrate Christ's good works. It was a mixture of pop culture and religion. It was perfect for a postwar America longing for an anchor, seeking a return to the values that elevate. Youth for Christ emphasized the healing power of Christ and the promise that a Christian life held out to young people across America after the devastating war.

Across the United States and Canada, and later in Europe, Saturday-night rallies of young people sprang up independently of the churches. With jukeboxes blaring the latest tunes and teens jitterbugging their nights away, with boys sporting broad-shouldered suits and girls their baggy sweaters and bobby sox, the groups filled a cultural niche, especially in major cities where large numbers of young people and returning servicemen had been dislocated by the war. The meetings were fun with a serious purpose. Informal and mostly held in secular auditoriums, the emphasis was on community singing, from gospel tunes to Negro spirituals. Musical groups performed, and at the end a youthful preacher gave a brief religious talk. Although the thrust was pietistic, it was more show business than religion.

Inspired by the youth evangelism work of men such as Jack Wyrtzen, a former jazz musician from New York; Charles Templeton, a highly literate yet explosive orator from Toronto, Canada; and Torrey Johnson, a preacher from Chicago, a number of youth leaders from around the country met at Winona Lake, Indiana, in 1945 to form a temporary organization to serve as a national channel for the various rallies. The following year, 42 delegates from the various groups met again at Winona Lake to make Youth for Christ International (YFCI) into a permanent organization. Torrey Johnson was elected president.

Johnson was an entertainer and entrepreneur of the first order. Round-faced, with hair parted exactly in the middle that fell in dark waves, he was a great talker. Although he was in the religion business, he was not an accomplished preacher. Still, he was brimming with schemes and promotions, and the religious business always needed promoters. A Chicagoan, a student at the Moody Bible Institute, and a graduate of Wheaton College, Johnson was pastor of the Midwest Bible Church in Chicago. He also began a radio program called *Chapel Hour* that aired on a local station. This show would later be broadcast by the newly formed ABC radio network under the name *Songs in the Night*, a show that Billy Graham would one day host.

In the early 1940s, Johnson hit upon a scheme to popularize evangelical Christianity among Chicago's youth. With the help of a number of fellow students from Chicago, such as Stratton Shufelt and Bob Cook, and with the assistance of Dr. V. Raymond Edman and other established church figures in the Chicago area, Johnson launched Chicago's Youth for Christ. He did it with little money but with much exuberance. Many in the Youth for Christ movement were new to the preaching business, some with little more than experience in a young people's society or Sunday school. They were a fresh group, and Johnson encouraged innovation, spontaneity, and a spirit to take chances for God.

Torrey Johnson's biggest recruit was Billy Graham, whom he had heard on the radio. Johnson offered Graham 75 dollars a week plus expenses to be Youth for Christ's first field representative. Graham saw the offer as an opportunity for an adventure, a splendid chance to show off his best skills and be at the forefront of a novel experiment in the Lord's work. Billy would give up the pastorate at the small church in Western Springs. He would now serve the Lord onstage in a pastel suit, with shiny socks that appeared to glow in the dark, loud ties, and pomaded hair. He would be backed by impresarios, girl trios, magicians, huge choirs, swing-band instrumentalists, and even a horse named MacArthur who would kneel at the cross and tap his hoof 12 times, signifying the number of Christ's apostles. One memorable performance included a sonata for 100 pianos.

The Youth for Christ movement was scintillating. Soon, even such venues as New York City's Madison Square Garden couldn't hold all the young people who wanted to attend.

On stage in Chicago, at the first rally in which he was to speak, Graham sat uncomfortably, as a huge audience of several thousand loomed in the front. Billy looked around, leaned over to a friend, and said that he was scared to death. A 1,000-voice choir was arranged behind the massive platform. Above, a banner trumpeted: CHICAGOLAND YOUTH FOR CHRIST. If Graham was scared, it didn't show once he got behind the microphone. He spoke vigorously for twenty minutes, giving an invitation for converts to come forward—and many did.

William Randolph Hearst, the aging newspaper tycoon, was so enthralled with the Youth for Christ movement that he invited the group to spend a weekend with him at his fabled Xanadu mansion in San Simeon, California. Although the Youth for Christ team had to decline the invitation, Hearst continued to lavish praise on their efforts. His nationwide chain of newspapers had, over the years, become quite skillful not only at delivering the news but at promoting it. He and his chain were great manipulators of public opinion, especially for causes that fit Hearst's conservative political philosophy and pro-American bias. He saw in Youth for Christ a poster group for Americanism: clean-cut young people on the trail for the religion of the people. What better group to represent America abroad, to show off the fabric of its culture and, indeed, to face down communism?

At a Youth for Christ rally in Seattle, a Hearst photographer prowled the grounds shooting picture after picture. After the rally, two reporters cornered one of the preachers and did a two-hour interview. The next morning, a three-page spread on the rally in the Seattle *Post Intelligencer* greeted readers, including color photos. The Hearst empire was revving up the promotion machines. When William Randolph Hearst began to pull the levers of his considerable power, there were repercussions. Numerous magazines, such as *Time, Newsweek,* and *Maclean's,* did stories, and *Life* magazine even hired a reporter to follow Youth for Christ.

Torrey Johnson later said of Hearst: "He saw what happened in Chicago Stadium when thirty thousand people attended a rally. He heard about what was going on across America and how this thing was spreading through servicemen to different parts of the world. I think he may have had a two-fold motive. On the one hand he may have had, and I like to think he had, a good motive of doing something helpful for his own country. He was a great patriot. He was a loyal American. He supported those causes that he felt were...that held traditional American values. So I like to think at that...from one point of view he wanted to help. On the other point of view, I think he saw the possibility of widening the circulation of his newspaper." Johnson saw a telegram that had been sent to one of Hearst's papers with the order to "Puff Youth for Christ."[1]

From Boston and New York to Seattle and Los Angeles, the Hearst papers, as Johnson said, "puffed big." Wire services across the country and in Europe picked up on the phenomenon.

In his first year alone, Graham traveled over 200,000 miles and, incredibly, spoke in 47 states. He and his companions got to know very well every inch of DC-3 airplanes. Graham, however, found a lifelong fellow worker not so far from home. At a rally in Asheville, North Carolina, 15 miles from Montreat, where he and Ruth had spent their honeymoon, he persuaded song leader Cliff Barrows to join the team.

A former songster for evangelist Jack Shuler, Barrows had received a degree in Sacred Music and Shakespearean Drama from Bob Jones College. A cheerful crowd rouser with a wide, ever-present smile, Barrows became an important ingredient in the mix of personalities that Graham and others in Youth for Christ were assembling. Like so many others who joined Graham and became personally close to him, Barrows never left his side for very long.

Music was at the heart of the rallies. There were musical groups of all kinds—trios, choirs, instrumental combinations, even a group of nine girls, chosen as much for their beauty as for their voices, called "Youth for Christ Octette." The first cornetist in the Toronto Symphony formed a trumpet trio. In New York, Jack Wyrtzen, the ex–jazz musician turned religious promoter, held musical rallies that were carried on radio and sent around the world on short wave. All of this musical entertainment was somewhat ironical for Graham. One of his close friends said once that Billy was tone deaf and to stand by him while he was singing was something of a dizzying experience.

The rallies were grand spectacles. In Toronto, the choir, a thousand strong, dressed in white except for a few individuals in the middle who wore black, formed the outline of a cross. There were five grand pianos; a pageant of individuals dressed in the full costumes of countries from around the world; the girl Octette; and tiny five-year-old Tommy Ambrose, who could belt out the old Negro spiritual song "Dem bones, dem bones, dem dry bones," better than any other tiny five year old in the world and invariably brought the house down. A huge mob of teenagers followed the group out of the arena, jamming the concourse, cheering and singing. Billy and Templeton had to climb onto the marble balustrades to speak to them.

With Billy constantly on the road, Ruth lived for a time with her parents in Montreat. Billy and Ruth would soon purchase and remodel a house across the street from the Bells. The two families would thus forge an even closer bond. The location close to her parents was comforting for Ruth during her husband's long absences. Although Graham was on the road almost constantly and received a small salary, Ruth, with her relatives nearby, seemed content. She believed firmly in the work her husband had undertaken and was determined to help his career flourish.

In September 1945 Ruth gave birth to Virginia Leftwich Graham. The Bells gave her the nickname of Gigi, the Chinese word for little sister. She was the first of the five Graham children who would grow up in Montreat.

In early 1946, a Youth for Christ evangelistic team, including Johnson, Graham, Templeton, and Stratton Shufelt, traveled on a three-week tour of Great Britain. Wes Hartzell, staff writer for Hearst's Chicago *Herald-American*, traveled with the group along with a reporter and photographer for *Life*. Over 1,000 Chicagoland Youth for Christ members saw them off at the airport. As Graham, Johnson, and Templeton kneeled on the tarmac in prayer, photographers snapped photos. Templeton later said it had the feel of Alice in Wonderland, with the three of them praying and the crouching photographers yelling out "Keep praying, fellas!"

En route to England, the tour group became stranded by weather overnight at a Newfoundland air force base. The base's social director, spying this extraordinary group dressed in excessively colorful garb, assumed they were a vaudeville act. Torrey Johnson, ever eager for an audience, did not disabuse him of that notion. The officer invited the group to appear before his troops.

As Templeton walked on the stage, the applause was loud and raucous. All the seats were filled with servicemen and others jammed the aisles and lined the walls. Templeton told a few lame jokes and drew respectable laughter. He introduced Stratton Schufelt who did an up-tempo version of "Short'nin Bread" to middling applause. When Templeton appeared again, told a few more jokes, and then tried to introduce Torrey Johnson, identifying him as the head of Youth for Christ, the servicemen began to look at each other. "The crowd suddenly looked puzzled and the booing began interspersed with cries of 'Bring on the girls!'" Templeton later remembered. "After a minute or two, Torrey abandoned whatever he had in mind, made his exit, and I was back onstage. Shouting over the chaos, I brought on Stratt for his second song, 'The Old Rugged Cross.' Even with the microphone he was inaudible in the din. The crowd had turned ugly and was shouting and booing. Backstage, Torrey was saying, 'Hey—we're doing great! Go out there Chuck and introduce Billy.' I refused, but having no option, again faced the hooting mob. Billy gave it a valiant try but it was a lost battle."[2]

Despite the air force base fiasco, Youth for Christ was an enormous hit in Europe. The team held meetings in overflowing churches and halls in London, some of which had barely withstood German attacks. The tour continued to York and Manchester and then on to Scotland, with appearances in Glasgow, Aberdeen, and Edinburgh. Sporting their loud sports jackets and bow ties, they seemed a curiosity among a people recovering from a long struggle.

This young preacher whose words shot out at machine-gun pace—so fast it was somewhat difficult to understand everything he said, especially with the American South accent—fascinated them. People who listened to his delivery sometimes felt as if they needed to take breaths for him. He was rousing and full of spirit, a dose of refreshing energy. With each new trip to the evangelist platform, Graham's preaching developed and matured, resonating with increased power and authority.

The British people, still living on food rations and just beginning the struggle to rebuild, profoundly moved Billy. On some occasions, he spoke in partially rebuilt churches so filled with fog rolling through their open spaces that he could not see all of the audience.

Canon Tom Livermore, an Anglican cleric, became an important contact for Youth for Christ and for Graham in England. Livermore invited Billy to preach in an Anglican church wearing clerical robes. Billy did so with a bright tie showing from underneath. Torrey Johnson remembered how Livermore returned from the service and "described to us enthusiastically how he preached in the robes and so forth. But he gave an invitation, and a large group of people responded to the invitation that night in Tom Livermore's church. Tom Livermore came to see us afterward, and he was enthused about what happened."[3]

Graham wanted to return to England, and the associates he had met there wanted very much to have him there again, this time for a longer period. Later that year, Graham and Cliff Barrows did return, and Ruth joined them for part of the trip. They stayed six months, some of it during a frigid winter; many times they slept with their clothes on in rooms that had little heat. Graham and Barrows spoke all across Great Britain, establishing friendships that would last a lifetime.

A MINISTRY OF HIS OWN

By May 1948, when Ruth gave birth to the second of the Graham children, Anne Morrow Graham, the 30-year-old evangelist was beginning to see that his ministry could be something special. He told Torrey Johnson, "Torrey, God's given me one great gift. I have a gift of bringing people to Christ. And that I've got to do."[4]

At 30 years of age, Billy Graham was, Charles Templeton said, "a thin, gangling six-foot-two with a thatch of blonde wavy hair (he wore a baseball cap in private to keep it from mounding too high). He had a lean, angular face, a wide mouth, a square jaw, and jutting eyebrows above a hawk nose. The denim-blue eyes seemed more intense for being surrounded by dark circles. He was not as handsome as he would be with the addition of a dozen years. On a platform, despite an impression of immaturity, he had a commanding presence and a strong, flexible voice."[5]

It was in this early period of Graham's professional career that he made a critical decision about belief. One of his friends remarked to him that recent scientific discoveries and the inherent contradictions within biblical accounts of creation had undermined the Bible's assertion that the Earth was created in a few days. Graham discounted his friend's remark, saying that he had discovered in his own ministry that when he took the Bible literally, proclaimed it to be God's word, and did not question either its authenticity or accuracy, he felt its power over him and his audiences. He had decided, he said, to abandon further speculation on biblical accuracy. He did not have the time or the intellect to wrestle with such questions, he said, and had decided once and for all to stop questioning. It was a startling admission to his friend. Graham, in no uncertain terms, had abandoned further intellectual inquiry, at least in questions involving the Bible.

In 1947, William Bell Riley, founder and president of Northwestern Schools, institutions known for the evangelical training of hundreds of ministers and missionaries over the years, retired. He asked Billy Graham to be his successor.

Riley had served as pastor of the First Baptist Church of Minneapolis, Minnesota, for over 50 years. A gifted orator, he was a dean of fundamental, evangelical Christianity and throughout his career conducted big-time evangelistic campaigns. In 1942 he had retired from the pastorate to devote his time to Northwestern Schools, which he had founded many years earlier. Northwestern was recognized as a fundamentalist bastion, a school that promised to educate young people to resist the poisonous, pagan teachings of modern science and evolution and to resist also the teachings of Catholic, Jewish, and other faiths that he regarded as reprehensible. Riley, who had seen Graham preach on a number of occasions, recognized him as a rising evangelist star and personally asked Billy to take over the reins as president.

Although Graham was reluctant, Riley was persuasive, and Graham accepted. When Riley died several months later, Graham suddenly became the school's president. At age 29, he was the youngest college president in the United States.

Graham began to see Northwestern as becoming another Wheaton, an internationally known, first-class religious school. He asked boyhood friend T. W. Wilson to be vice president. Born in 1918 in Charlotte, Wilson had been a close friend of Graham since boyhood. Taking a somewhat different career road than did Graham, Wilson had been ordained a Southern Baptist minister in 1939, had earned a degree in religion at Bob Jones University, and had pursued graduate work at the University of Alabama. He would finally earn a doctorate at Bob Jones University. Wilson had not intended to follow in Graham's footsteps; his own career as an evangelist was promising. Nevertheless, when Graham approached him in 1948 about taking the job at Northwestern Schools, Wilson could not turn down his old friend. Billy convinced him that by building a formidable team they could together better serve the Lord. For Graham, the presidency thus became essentially part-time, as the evangelist continued to take on invitations to preach. T. W. remained in Minnesota to take care of the administrative work of running the institution.

Due to Graham's highly visible career in Youth for Christ, he made an immediate impact on the school. Many of the younger Youth for Christ members who were ready to enter college suddenly changed plans and headed for Northwestern, thus increasing the enrollment significantly in the first years of Graham's presidency.

Graham remained president of Northwestern Schools until 1952. By the time of his resignation, Graham had received several honorary doctorate degrees from religious schools. He would leave Northwestern not only with experience but also with a title he could add to his name—"Doctor."

Graham personally felt he left Northwestern in much better condition than he found it. During his tenure, enrollment rose sharply, new buildings appeared on campus, a two-wave radio station opened, and the college magazine (the *Northwestern Pilot*) achieved a circulation of 35,000. His years at Northwestern gave him an invaluable glimpse into the issues of finance, promotion, and administration. Although he was never talented in any of these areas, he surrounded himself with associates who were. They taught him to delegate responsibility, to tap the right sources of advice, and how to create a team.

Several of the staff and faculty at Northwestern later joined Graham's evangelistic organization. Minneapolis would become the headquarters for Billy's worldwide ministry.

It was at this time that Graham began to hold revival meetings on his own during breaks from Youth for Christ and absences from the college. His individual ministry gradually grew, and with it Graham's vision for the possibilities the future might hold. His calling, he now believed, was not as a pastor, not as an administrator of a college, not as a member of Youth for Christ preaching to a limited audience. Billy's vision for himself and his ministry was much larger. His early successes convinced him that he could gather a team, conduct rallies on his own, and follow in the pattern of other great evangelists who preached to the masses. He eventually left both the college and Youth for Christ in order to follow that calling.

In November 1948, while in Modesto, California, he gathered close advisers, including Grady and T. W. Wilson, Cliff Barrows, and Bev Shea, to ask their advice about the future of the evangelistic enterprise. Billy Graham had read Sinclair Lewis's 1927 novel *Elmer Gantry*, which told the story of an unscrupulous clergyman who doubted the sacred truths he preached and also had led a sordid personal life. The novel outraged clergymen across the country, including one from a western state, who suggested that Lewis be hanged, and another from the east, who merely wanted him jailed for assailing the ministry. The novel had enough resonance to make Graham eager to avoid any circumstances that might besmirch his own career in a manner similar to the story of Reverend Gantry.

Graham knew how numerous evangelists, not just those who appeared in novels, had succumbed to the lure of money and power; how their careers had been shattered and their good names ridiculed and scorned. He and his closest advisers decided to institute a formal bond to insulate the Billy Graham ministry from those temptations and to protect it from even the appearance of impropriety.

Later, they called their plan the "Modesto Manifesto." It became the centerpiece of Graham's organization, the standard by which the members pledged to operate. The group decided to incorporate as a nonprofit organization with trustees who were not family members. Graham worked for a set salary, not for "love offerings" traditionally handed out to evangelist preachers. In order to avoid the appearance of competing with local pastors, the group decided to visit a city only if it received an invitation by the religious community. At that early meeting in Modesto, Graham and his associates set a pattern for financial accountability that would direct operations for years to come. In addition, the group charted a careful, if rather unusual and extreme, strategy to ensure that the evangelist would not be tainted by even the suspicion of sexual impropriety. From that point on, Graham would make it a point not to travel, meet, or dine alone with any woman other than Ruth.

THE LOS ANGELES CRUSADE

In 1949, a group called "Christ for Greater Los Angeles" invited the evangelist to their city for a series of rallies. They had secured a spot on the outskirts of the city and would erect what would be known as the "Canvas Cathedral." With little press coverage and sparse crowds, the Canvas Cathedral hardly seemed promising.

When Billy Graham came to Los Angeles, accompanied by Ruth, he already had an admirer waiting. William Randolph Hearst, the newspaper magnate, had followed Graham's preaching with Youth for Christ. His writers and photographers had accompanied Graham and the others to England and other countries and fawned over the young Christian entertainers. Now that Graham was a traveling evangelist on his own with the gusto and talent that Hearst had recognized from early on, the aging newspaper king was ready again to lend a hand. He told his reporters to hype the Los Angeles tent meetings. They did. When the Hearst papers filled column after column with news about the new evangelist star, competing papers in numerous cities followed suit.

Graham got an additional boost. Stuart Hamblen, a Texan cowboy who was already a radio legend on the West Coast, took an interest in the Graham crusade and invited the evangelist to appear on his program, promising that with his endorsement the tent would fill. Billy eagerly accepted.

When Hamblen, a confessed alcoholic, announced on the air that he would attend one of the rallies; indeed, the tent was packed. Hamblen was so moved by the service and Graham's call for redemption that he marched down the aisle with other converts and later gave up drinking. With the news that Stuart Hamblen had converted at a Billy Graham crusade, the airwaves buzzed, and the lines entering the rallies grew long.

Graham's Los Angeles tent revival had became a national happening. Ads trumpeted the news: "Greater L.A.'s Greatest Revival Continues!" and "Billy Graham's 5th Sin-Smashing Week! From all Southern California points, thousands have flocked to hear America's outstanding young evangelist—BILLY GRAHAM 30 year-old college president who has become famous as the Billy Sunday of the mid-twentieth century."[6]

"A standing room only audience was on hand yesterday," the *Los Angeles Times* reported. "At the afternoon service an estimated 1500 persons of those converted during the revival walked forward to the preacher's platform in response to the invitation."[7]

If the trappings were circus-like at the giant tent at Washington Boulevard and Hill Street, the message was still as sobering as ever. This was, indeed, a stern God that Graham presented, a kind of soul policeman, investigating every impure thought and action, spying on every moment of a person's life. "And God is going to have proof of everything you ever did," declared Graham. "He will know about that night years ago which you've forgotten. Every idle word that we have said—every curse word, every swear word, every lie, will be recorded in His book. All those things that you covered up and hid as secret, God says, are going to be brought to life and the whole world will know and you'll stand there with perspiration dripping down your cheeks and with your eyes rolling in fear. The question on the judgment day will be 'What did you do with Jesus?'"[8]

Graham introduced another prominent theme at the Los Angeles revival, a theme that would be increasingly dominant as his career progressed—the threat of communism. Two days before the opening night of the revival, President Harry S. Truman announced what was essentially the beginning of the arms race with the Soviet Union. The Russians had successfully tested the atomic bomb, Truman declared, and had been building a nuclear arsenal for some time.

Graham seized on the issue, contrasting the Christian democracy of the United States to the godless dictatorship of the Soviet Union. The lines were drawn—good versus evil; God versus the devil; democracy versus communism. To be a Christian was to be a patriotic American. Communism was running rampant in Los Angeles and across the United States, fumed Graham. Only a religious revival, a war against the devil's instrument, communism, could satisfy God's judgment hand.

It is not surprising that many left the tabernacle trembling. Many of the converted were undoubtedly frightened down the sawdust trail by such threats of divine retribution. The preacher was speaking to each and every one in that tabernacle, no matter where they sat, no matter how small they might have tried to make themselves in their seats. They were like the teenage Billy had been years ago before the stern warnings of the evangelist Mordecai Ham. God knew all of their secrets, Billy told the crowds as Ham had done, and they would have to repent, each one of them, or face the consequences.

If the world was teetering still on the edge of oblivion, whose fault was it? It certainly wasn't the fault of God. If there was fear of atomic warfare and economic, social, and political, problems; if there was moral degeneration running rampant, it was not the fault of God. It was the fault of those who had not yet taken the step of repentance. "That old time religion," one Los Angles reporter said, "has gone as modern as an atomic bomb in the thunderous revival meetings that Rev. Billy Graham conducts nightly.... Nothing detracts from the traditional fury and power of an old-fashioned gospel gathering. That's what his listeners, many of whom remember with pleasure the late Billy Sunday, want. And that's what they get."[9]

Besides Stuart Hamblen, other Los Angeles celebrities attended the rallies and met informally with Graham, including actors Jane Russell,

Jimmy Stewart, and Spencer Tracy. Even underworld gangster Mickey Cohen commented favorably on the effects of the Los Angeles crusade.

In six weeks, 200,000 people gathered at the tent, pouring in at the rate of 10,000 a night to listen to Graham tell such simple stories as this: An irreligious business man lost his family, his self-respect, and his standing in his community. He was a beaten and discouraged individual. At a revival he repented and was led by the revival counselors to a small tent for an interview. As he approached the counselor he realized it was his former wife, whom he had not seen since their divorce 10 years earlier. The story ends, not surprisingly, with their remarriage.

The Graham team extended the crusade from its original intended length of three weeks to eight. Still, the crowds filled the tent. Finally, the organizers and participants, drained financially and physically, could continue no longer. An exhausted Graham, who had lost 20 pounds from his already lean frame and had preached all the sermon material he had more than once, was careful not to take personal credit for the astounding success of the crusade. It was, he said, all the work of God.

On November 20, 1949, nearly two months after it began, the Los Angeles crusade closed. Through his own organizing zeal and platform presence, through the powerful hand of the media and more than a little luck, Billy Graham had catapulted into a fame that would carry him into the decade of the fifties.

NOTES

1. Torrey Johnson, interview by Robert Shuster, (CN285.T4), Archives of the Billy Graham Center, Wheaton College, Wheaton, Ill., 13 February 1984.

2. Charles Templeton, "An Anecdotal Memoir: Chapter Inside Evangelism: Touring with Youth for Christ and Billy Graham," http://www.templetons.com/charles/memoir/evang-graham.html.

3. Torrey Johnson, interview by Robert Shuster, (CN285.T6), Archives of the Billy Graham Center, Wheaton College, Wheaton, Ill., 14 August 1985.

4. Torrey Johnson, interview by Robert Shuster, 13 February 1984.

5. Templeton, "Anecdotal Memoir."

6. Advertisement from a Los Angeles newspaper, (Collection 360, Scrapbook 5), Archives of the Billy Graham Center, Wheaton College, Wheaton, Ill., November 1949.

7. *Los Angeles Times*, 14 November 1949.

8. Graham, *Revival in Our Time*, pp. 133–39.

9. *Los Angeles Daily News*, 30 September 1949.

Chapter 5

A REVIVALIST HERITAGE: THE GREAT AWAKENING TO BILLY SUNDAY

Revivalism was rooted in the country's religious and emotional fiber even before the American Revolution. Gospel preachers, infused with a calling to spread the biblical word, carried little more on their mules and horses than their few belongings and small tents as they traveled the backwoods, clearing spots for camp meetings. They saw themselves as God's messengers, appointed to bring wayward sinners to their senses, to save souls for Christ. They called for the masses to be infused with the spirit, to be swept away in a religious cleansing.

In the mid-1700s, a phenomenon later called The Great Awakening swept over the American colonies, a mass psychological outburst of religious ardor involving thousands. Men and women engaged in bizarre emotional testimonies, often shrieking and howling uncontrollably, apparently gripped by religious convulsions. Itinerant preachers pointed to the phenomenon as proof that the Lord was at work in the colonies and exhorted others to yield to the power of the Holy Spirit and the joys of salvation. They disregarded much of the established clergy, who dared question the legitimacy of these religious conversions. The pastors were, many said, totally out of step, mired in murky theology and lacking any connection with true religious feeling. It was in the spirit of the revival that God was showing his power, not in catechisms, intellectual quibbling over scripture, or piddling prayer.

There was Jonathan Edwards, a New Englander, delivering frightening disquisitions on good and evil, sin and punishment. There was George Whitefield, drawing huge crowds to hear his vivid stories of the lurking serpents of hell and how to defeat them. Benjamin Franklin once said that

Whitefield's voice could reach 30,000 people. The good doctor set out to prove his thesis by standing a half-mile away as the renowned evangelist blared out his message. Franklin heard his words. So did thousands of others caught up in religious fervor.

A revivalist passing through New London, Connecticut, invited the population to assemble at the wharf the following afternoon and to bring with them many of their needless worldly belongings as a sacrifice to the Lord. That evening, with hallelujahs and delirium abounding, a great bonfire rose in New London, fired by gowns, wigs, books, men's suits, and all other manner of personal possessions.

To many traditional church leaders, such practices were heathen, and the revivalist preachers merely hucksters out to attract attention and fame. Menasseh Cutler, a Massachusetts Congregationalist clergyman, was so outraged after listening to traveling evangelist John Leland that he went on a rant: "Such a farrago, bawled with stunning voice, horrid tone, frightful grimaces, and extravagant gestures, I believe, was never heard by any decent auditory."[1] The whole performance, he said, was an affront to religion itself as well as common decency.

In the early years of the nineteenth century, new revival leaders took the place of their forbearers. They came from various religious backgrounds—Presbyterians, Baptists, Methodists, and other less well-known sects. They rode frontier routes through mountains and valleys, setting up camp meetings to gather worshippers. At the meetings, it was often reported, people fell so violently under the spell of religious zeal that they would writhe on the ground, groaning. Others would sit rigidly frozen in place. Others moaned or wailed endlessly. Spurring on the whole scene was the revivalist preacher, shouting for the faithful to trust their inner wellsprings of religious power. Let out the psychological torment; express the joy. Fight the devil with raw emotional force.

The battles over the validity of revivalism in American society flared over the years. In each generation, there were towering figures around whom large numbers of followers rallied. In the early part of the nineteenth century, there was Lyman Beecher. The son of a prosperous Connecticut farmer, he was educated at Yale University. Beecher became a fiery religious figure who took on the established clergy. Like other evangelists, he began to see himself as an instrument of God, anointed to take on the crusty religious establishment and stoke the fires of a new resurgence of faith. "The Lord drove me but I was ready," he proclaimed. The preacher talked of terrible plagues and earthquakes, God's acts of vengeance that would rain down on a people unwilling to join the crusade. American society was rotting, Beecher believed, and the best way to win God's assurance of salvation was in good works—ridding society of drunkenness and vice, restoring honesty in government, and promoting charities.

There was Charles Grandison Finney, riding through western New York and neighboring states preaching that the destinies of individuals lay in their own hands, that lives were not predestined by God as claimed by many clergymen. "Sinners Bound to Change Their Own Hearts," his most famous sermon, laid the responsibility clearly on the shoulders of each individual to play a vital part in their own salvation. A stirring orator with an icy glare, Finney, some said, had an hypnotic effect on his listeners, pointing directly to individuals in the audience, challenging them face to face to confess their shortcomings and take vital steps to change their lives.

Both Beecher and Finney looked to a moral army to reform society and promote the public good. If Christians could wage war against evil and corruption, it would demonstrate a commitment to God's commands. By the 1830s all manner of volunteer organizations and societies fought against alcohol, Sabbath-breaking, and the brutal treatment of children. They promoted education for women. Evangelists often spearheaded these campaigns, warriors leading their Christian troops against Satan, purifying society.

Nevertheless, there were always the detractors. They attacked the evangelist preachers as hucksters and cheap promoters who traded on the Christian message for personal fame and money. Editorialists, politicians, established ministers—all who felt threatened by the revivalist energy and its success—fought back, warning those who were attracted by the revivals that they were being conned and tricked. These were not God's messengers, they charged, but the devil's playmates. The religious hysteria and spontaneous spiritual rebirth were nothing but emotionalism run amok. It was not God's spirit at all, but the delusions of misguided fools.

After the Civil War, horseback-riding evangelists, armed with their stock sermons, rode from town to town spreading the word. Surrender to Christ and be saved, they implored their listeners; join with others in the crowd to announce your spiritual rebirth. Like masses gathering at circuses, crowds swarmed into the revival tents. To be born again could be as easy as losing yourself in the frenzy. Join your neighbors and change your life.

In the late nineteenth century, the towering evangelistic figure in America was a man who had given up a promising shoe business to enter the Christian ministry. Dark and swarthy in appearance, the relatively uneducated Dwight Moody had worked his way to the presidency of the Chicago YMCA through tremendous vigor and determination, charging from one religious activity to another. He traveled the country and the world delivering powerful sermons and moved the focus of the revival from small towns and backwoods areas to large cities. He was the first to introduce sophisticated business acumen and strategy to evangelism. At a time when American industry learned to mass-produce steel and automobiles, Dwight Moody began to mass-produce religion. From his careful selection of musical groups and his production of hymnals to his energetic, organized advertising campaigns, Moody developed a revival empire. It is estimated that Moody traveled more than a million miles and addressed more than 100 million people, all in an age without airplanes or microphones.

Like many evangelists before and after him, Moody was not a sophisticated biblical scholar or even a careful student. His message was informal and simple—renounce sin; accept redemption by Christ. He swore allegiance to no particular religious denomination or sect, disdaining theological disputes as counterproductive to a resurgence of religious enthusiasm. This was a simple battle, he believed, between Satan and God, and bickering between various Christian denominations was a distraction. He lamented the divisions within the Christian family and longed for the day all division would cease, when Roman Catholics and Protestants would see eye to eye and march together.

To Moody, the impulse to cleanse society of its ills that so consumed Beecher and Finney was also misguided and essentially a waste of time. "I look upon this world as a wrecked vessel," Moody declared in one of his oft-quoted statements. Darkness and ruin were already upon the land. Only Christ's second coming would cleanse the world. For now, individuals must repent and give their lives to personal salvation.

As Dwight Moody dominated the turn-of-the-century revivalist stage from his base in Chicago, Billy Sunday was playing center field for the Chicago White Stockings. He was born in Iowa, the son of a Union soldier who died shortly before Billy was born. He spent most of his early years on a small Iowa farm owned by his grandfather.

Baseball rescued Billy Sunday and made him nationally famous. The famous first baseman and manager of the Chicago White Stockings, Cap Anson, saw Billy play baseball in Iowa as a teenager and recruited him for the big leagues. He was the fastest player in the major leagues, so fast that the White Stockings sometimes arranged for match races between Billy and track stars. Unfortunately, he couldn't hit. At a time when batting averages often reached .400, Billy's lifetime mark was .254. One scribe quipped, "If only he could steal first!"

A few years into his baseball career, Sunday wandered half-drunk into the Pacific Garden Mission in Chicago. These were the days of open vice in Chicago, the days of the famous Levee district with its gambling parlors, dope dens, cheap grind shows, and splendid illicit houses. Religious groups sometimes invaded the Levee to fight all of this. On that night in 1883, Billy was profoundly moved by the revival service. He later said, "I've followed Jesus from that day to this very second, like the hound on the trail of the fox."[2] After a few more frustrating years at the plate Billy gave up swinging at those exasperating curve balls and joined the YMCA as an assistant secretary. Later, he joined the evangelist J. Wilbur Chapman and developed the unique speaking abilities and stage mannerisms that propelled a remarkable preaching career.

He was ordained by the Chicago Presbytery in 1903. He began his revival life in small gospel meetinghouses in Iowa. He soon graduated to small churches and tents and quickly became the most exciting national evangelist since the great Dwight Moody, whose career had flourished in the last decades of the nineteenth century. Dwight Moody, however, had never captured an audience like Billy Sunday.

Within a few years, the famous baseball player–turned–evangelist began to fill large city tabernacles. His performances were strikingly unconventional, even in the world of revival hoopla. With a huge supporting cast of choirs and skilled musicians, Billy was a commanding presence, leaping about the stage, slapping his hands, crashing his fists on chairs. A photographic memory enabled him to reel off long sermons that were always punctuated by colorful homilies and common slang. At the close of his services, converts would parade up the aisles to testify to their spiritual rebirth, a phenomenon known as "hitting the sawdust trail."

Sunday's conservative theology was like a moral scoreboard: good things to do versus sins to avoid. He venerated hard work, godly living, and the holiness of motherhood; he condemned sin, vanity, scientists, liberals and radicals, booze, novel reading, theaters, paying too much attention to pet animals, and many other amusements. He did not, however, condemn baseball.

By 1912, Billy Sunday had become a national religious phenomenon. His simple message of sin and repentance and his acrobatic stage mannerisms rocketed him to national fame. He would shadowbox the devil, pretend to pick up giant boulders and hurl them into the crowd, and slide like a ballplayer crossing home plate. His words came easily, rhythmically, and the moods rolled and shifted. His message was not one of dainty, lily-livered piety but of hard-muscled, pickaxed religion, a religion from the gut. Prayer was a manly duty; faith was mountain-moving, galvanic. The tough guys were on the side of God.

To millions across the country, Sunday was God's mouthpiece. He had big choirs and great musicians such as trombonist Homer Rodeheaver, who stayed with Billy for nearly two decades. This was a time of dizzying change in society, a time of labor problems, crime, cities choking in poverty, and masses of immigrants pouring into the country. It was a time of attacks against capitalism, against religion, against tradition.

Billy especially enjoyed attacking Protestant ministers who had weak backbones in attacking sin and who rolled over weakly in the face of the country's enemies. He called them "fudge-eating mollycoddles" and hypocrites. Billy loved to take on hypocrites. "I can skin a hypocrite," he thundered, "salt his hide, and tack it on a barn door to dry before you are puckering your old mouth to spit on your whetstone to start to sharpen your jack knife to begin the operation!"[3]

It was in the context of this long history of evangelical revivalism rooted in America's past that a young preacher from North Carolina packed his bags, memorized sermons, and headed to a small town for a revival. The names loomed large: Edwards, Whitefield, Beecher, Finney, Moody, and Sunday. They and their associates had carried the torch, sought converts in the wilderness. Seeing their calling and mission differently at times and often disagreeing on theological doctrine, they still combined to establish a tradition that carried through to the middle of the twentieth century, a tradition inherited by the gangling young man now ready to take on his own mission.

NOTES

1. Weisberger, *They Gathered at the River*, pp. 55–56.

2. Billy Sunday sermon, New York City campaign file, The Papers of Billy Sunday, Archives of the Billy Graham Center, Wheaton College, Wheaton, Ill., 1917.

3. Bruns, *Billy Sunday*, p. 121.

Chapter 6

THE LURE OF POWER AND POLITICS

With the onset of his national fame, people in high places wanted a piece of Billy Graham. Rich corporate executives, politicians, and others who saw benefit in an association with the evangelist began to hover. Convinced that he was personally acting as an agent of the Lord, Billy increasingly grasped at those offers of friendship and support, not in order to advance his own fame, he continually reminded others, but for the glory of God.

Following the Los Angeles publicity bonanza, Billy launched a two-week revival in Boston on December 31, 1949. Impressed by the news of the Los Angeles revival, Dr. Harold John Ockenga of Park Street Congregational Church in Boston, an evangelical church leader of great intellectual acumen who had gained national attention, promptly called Billy and suggested a revival. Vernon Patterson, a Graham associate, remembered the excitement: "Billy did come, and the first night the church was overcrowded. So they got Mechanics Hall and decided to prolong the meeting from...about ten days, I think. And there they...they...the Catholic press and others all began to play up Billy's meetings. So he'd already come into national prominence and everybody wanted to hear him and the newspapers, even the Catholic papers they...they all boosted that meeting."[1]

At a rally in Boston Garden, 16,000 people crammed inside, while thousands of others surrounded the old arena, hoping to catch a glimpse of the new celebrity in his loud sport coats and hand-painted ties, or just to take in the atmosphere. So confident in his own speaking prowess was the evangelist now that he took to dramatizing biblical stories and playing several characters. His slangy productions sometimes embarrassed his wife.

Graham held other meetings at Dr. Ockenga's Park Street Church and, by the time the revival had concluded, the evangelist enjoyed the support of over 70 churches. At a session of the Massachusetts House of Representatives, a young legislator named Thomas "Tip" O'Neill introduced Graham to the assembly. The Boston crowds at the rallies began to attract their own attention by singing hymns as they walked along the streets after Graham's sermons.

At the opening rally in Boston, Graham's sermon topic was "Will God Spare America." His conclusion was uncertain. Given mankind's sinful ways, Billy said he seriously doubted whether mankind would ever see the year 2000. This assertion gave the startled assemblage something to ponder.

Once again, the Graham revival bandwagon brought on new riders. Boston's Archbishop Richard Cushing printed "BRAVO BILLY" on the front of his diocesan paper during the rallies. Billy later said that the Boston rally and Cushing's endorsement made exceptional news across the country, especially among Catholic circles. It was the beginning of a wonderful friendship between the two prominent religious figures, Billy said, and it was the first time he had ever come to grips in any meaningful way with questions surrounding the relationship between those of the Protestant and Catholic faiths. He began to realize, he said, that there were different kinds of Christians. They might be called modernists, Catholics, or any denomination of Protestant, but they were all Christians and they were all doing the Lord's work.

Around the country the revival team scurried—Columbia, South Carolina; several New England states; all the way to Portland, Oregon. At each stop, Graham met influential civic and political leaders who, after the publicity he had gained in Los Angeles, seemed extraordinarily anxious to have him at their sides.

In South Carolina, Graham was a guest in the home of Governor Strom Thurmond, an ardent segregationist who had bolted the Democratic Party and run as an independent candidate for president in 1948. Thurmond delighted in Graham's company, introduced him to friends, and saw his own right-wing values as consistent with Graham's evangelistic campaigns. Thurmond provided a police escort to drive Graham and the team to several cities and towns in South Carolina for one-day meetings. Thurmond was the first of many political figures who courted and were in turn courted by Graham.

While a guest in Thurmond's mansion in Columbia, Graham met Henry Luce, the extremely wealthy publisher of *Time* and *Life* magazines. They talked for many hours. A son of Christian missionaries, Luce had earlier sent word to the Graham team that he wanted to meet Billy. Graham knew that Luce, much like William Randolph Hearst, held power at his fingertips to promote Graham's work internationally. They quickly established a friendship. "My interest lay not in the fact that *Time* and *Life* could give us an incredible amount of coverage," Billy said, "but that they could spread the word of evangelism to the ends of the world."[2]

It was a futile distinction that Graham continually attempted to make. If he was spreading evangelism to the ends of the world, he was also inevitably spreading his own fame and reputation to those same ends.

At the Columbia revival, Graham filled the University of South Carolina stadium with 40,000 listeners, including Thurmond and former Secretary of State James Byrnes. Luce's *Life* magazine reported: "For over an hour he held forth, arms waving, warning of a judgment day for all but the 'righteous in sinful America.'"[3]

Traveling back to Boston for an outdoor rally on Boston Common on April 23, 1950, Graham drew an estimated crowd of forty thousand, a rally that began in a hard rain. It was the largest throng in history to hear a prayer meeting at this famous site. Remembering that legendary New England evangelist George Whitefield had preached in 1740 on Boston Common, Graham borrowed from a Whitefield sermon on God in New England. By the time the sermon ended, the hard rain had stopped. Billy saw more in the change of the weather that day than sheer coincidence.

By the time of the Portland crusade in July 1950, it was clear that Billy Graham could be destined for an extraordinary career. The crowds, the press, the masses who gathered to hear him, the new contacts he was making among those in influential centers of power—all of it was gathering momentum at a speed that seemed almost dangerously out of control. As the evangelist's fame increased, so did criticism that he was an Elmer Gantry type who used evangelism to enrich himself personally. By the time the Portland crusade ended, for example, Grady Wilson had under his bed in a Portland hotel a shoebox that contained $25,000 in cash, checks, and pledges from the crowds who had responded to the offerings.

To counter these questions and complaints and to enable his ministry to run on an orderly, businesslike basis, the Graham team not only continued to abide by the financial and behavioral strictures to which they had pledged themselves in the Modesto Manifesto, but they also officially incorporated the Billy Graham Evangelistic Association (BGEA) as a nonprofit organization under the laws of the state of Minnesota. Its offices were set up in Minneapolis. Established in the fall of 1950, it became the sponsoring organization for the various Christian activities of Billy Graham. The organization would control and manage the complicated logistical and financial planning and accounting necessary for the increasingly large evangelist enterprise.

KOREA

On June 25, 1950, at 4 A.M., a tremendous artillery barrage hit the 1st Division of the Republic of Korea Army along the 38th parallel that divided North and South Korea. The invasion of South Korea by the North Korean Peoples' Army had begun.

The tensions between communist Russia and the United States following World War II had now reached a critical juncture. Should the United States, in its determination to stop the aggressive communist drive to take over all of Korea, now enter the conflict? American troops had been stationed in Korea after World War II, but the last unit pulled out in 1948. Only a military assistance group headquarters remained. South Koreans had been left to create their own armed forces, largely using equipment left behind by U.S. forces.

In 1950 Congress authorized $11 million in military aid to South Korea, but that money had not reached the South Koreans by the time of the attack. Meanwhile, the Russians, who defeated Japanese forces in Korea during World War II, had been arming and training the North Korean armed forces. Therefore, when the North Koreans attacked, their army vastly outnumbered the South Korean troops.

On June 27, 1950, President Truman made his decision. He announced that the Air Force and Navy would begin operations against the North Koreans. What he did not realize was that those operations would last over three years and that the conflict would be a quagmire in which more than 36,000 American troops would die. As the war slogged on in central Korea, the news each week of battles such as "Bloody Ridge" and "Heartbreak Ridge" would become familiar to Americans back home as the opposing forces battled back and forth over the same rugged terrain.

The fighting in Korea energized and gave substance to Billy Graham's message on communism. Those American boys losing their limbs and lives in the Far East were not fighting an abstraction, some vague fear of being overthrown by an evil totalitarian political system. They were fighting a real enemy who was firing real ammunition. With the hostilities in Korea raging, the battle against communism had taken on a physical dimension that could be readily understood by Americans as Billy Graham railed against the godless enemy.

A WHITE HOUSE FIASCO

By early July 1950, Graham's concentration on communism at his rallies had gained national attention. On July 14, Graham met in Washington with recently elected President Harry S. Truman. Representative John W. McCormack of Massachusetts had set up the visit after Graham's appearances in Boston. McCormack thought that an exchange of views between the president and the evangelist on such issues as the Communist threat, the Korean conflict, and the country's spiritual health would be enlightening for both. It did not quite work out that way.

The meeting itself was relatively uneventful, except for the overriding fact that this young evangelist, only a few years ago an unknown kid preacher for Youth for Christ, now found himself in the Oval Office with the president of the United States.

The president and Graham exchanged pleasantries, talked mostly about religion, and Billy, at his own suggestion, closed with a prayer. Following the meeting, Graham, dressed in a pistachio-green coat, kneeled with three of his associates on the lawn of the White House and prayed, while United Press International and Associated Press photographers shot pictures. The three men had just bought stylish, high quality white buck shoes made by the Florsheim Company of Chicago, the same brand they had seen Truman wearing. Together, Billy later admitted, they looked like a barbershop quartet. When reporters gathered to ask about the meeting, Billy talked about his personal conversation and his prayer with the president.

Truman was incensed. He was especially upset about Graham betraying the confidence of a private conversation, especially one involving such personal matters. Not only was Truman furious about the incident, he was unsparing in his criticism of the 31-year-old evangelist. He called him "counterfeit" and accused him of being a publicity-seeker, using others to advance his own fame. He made it clear that Billy and his team were no longer welcome at the White House. Graham was never invited back by Harry Truman.

Seemingly oblivious to possible reaction to the brazen, if not comical, scene on the White House lawn, Graham sent a letter thanking Truman for the visit, reminding the president of the vast crowds that were now flocking to every one of his services. Graham even had the temerity to advise Truman that a tough stance on communism would be in the best interests of the United States.

Years later, the image of Billy Graham was still clear in Truman's mind and the image was not a good one. It used to be, Truman said, that you could go out in the evening and run into a number of ranting evangelists working the crowds. Now, he said, there is only one, and he had, frankly, "gone off the beam." Truman saw only the publicity seeker in Graham, the slick pitchman poised to do anything to get ahead. "He was never a friend of mine," Truman once said, "I just don't go for people like that. All he's interested in is getting his name in the paper."[4]

If the president of the United States had little regard for the rising evangelist star, many others in positions of power were eager to join the Graham glory train. In 1951 Graham made the acquaintance of millionaire industrialist Russell Maguire, the Thompson submachine gun manufacturer. A committed anticommunist, backer of openly fascist organizations, and an anti-Semite, Maguire offered to give the evangelist a blank check for his work. Graham accepted a limited contribution of $75,000 to start a film ministry that in 1954 produced the movie *Oiltown, U.S.A.*

The central character in the film, Les Manning, has risen in the corporate world through power and money. Challenged by the Gospel during life's struggles, Manning finds that there is a greater power in the Lord. The film was one of many that the Billy Graham organization would produce over the years with the simple and direct message of sublimating one's presumption of personal power to the power of the Lord.

In February 1951, Graham for the first time preached in Fort Worth, Texas. It was in Fort Worth that he met oil baron Sid Richardson. The wealthy Texan saw the world as Billy Graham was seeing it. He saw communism looming. He believed that nuclear bombs in the hands of communists made doomsday imminent. He saw Hollywood and the recording studios turning out productions that he thought abandoned traditional American values.

A rabid Republican stalwart, Richardson was convinced that the country needed a Republican president for its very survival and he believed that only one candidate on the horizon could pull it off—General Dwight D. Eisenhower, the Commander at the Supreme Headquarters of the Allied Powers, stationed in Paris. Eisenhower's lack of political affiliation was an asset, Richardson believed. The problem facing Richardson was that Eisenhower seemed a reluctant candidate.

Mr. Sid, as Billy called him, asked the evangelist to assist him in encouraging Eisenhower to run. Graham declined to write Eisenhower directly. But Graham did send a letter to Richardson dated October 20, 1951, in which he said that unless America experienced a moral and spiritual reformation within the next two or three years, "we cannot possibly survive the severe tests that lie ahead." If Washington was not cleaned out, he said, there would be a period of chaos that could bring the country's downfall. "Sometimes I wonder who is going to win the battle first—the barbarians beating at our gates from without, or the termites of immorality from within. (I am praying) that God will guide you in the greatest decision of your life. Upon this decision could well rest the destiny of the Western World." He said that Church leaders across the nation must not sit idly by as they had in the past. Although Graham said he admired Senator Robert A. Taft, he was convinced that the unexciting Ohioan could not be elected. Only Dwight Eisenhower could prevail, he said. "There is only one man on the horizon with courage, honesty, integrity, and spiritual insight who has captured the imagination of the American people as no man in recent generations."[5]

Eisenhower told Richardson, "That was the damnedest letter I ever got. Who is this young fellow?" Years later, Graham admitted, "Nobody could accuse me of understatement."[6]

The general wrote to Graham on November 8, 1951, and marked it "Personal and confidential." He thanked the evangelist for the kind words and congratulated him on the evangelical work in which he was engaged. He hoped that Graham would "continue to press and fight for the old-fashioned virtues of integrity, decency, and straightforwardness in public life. I thank the Almighty that such inspired persons as yourself are ready and willing to give full time and energy to this great purpose."[7]

THE WASHINGTON CRUSADE

Billy Graham had once called Washington, D.C., "the most sinful city." His revival team decided to do something about it. In early 1952, the Graham crusade of the nation's capital was underway.

They were mostly ordinary people that attended the rallies in Washington, Graham said; but everywhere he went in the city, it seemed famous and powerful people sought him out. At evening prayer meetings at the National Guard Armory, two members of the House of Representatives volunteered as ushers. Vice President Alben Barkley told Billy, "You're certainly rockin' the old Capitol."

Graham held noontime prayer sessions in the Pentagon auditorium. "Never in my whole religious experience," he said, "have I seen such a hunger for religion as at the Pentagon." Eagerly responding to questions about the upcoming presidential election, Billy's sense of proportion and modesty gave way to growing self-absorption. He proclaimed that he hoped to meet every candidate for the presidency, including Harry Truman. It was as if he were at the center of a screening process. "I want to give them the moral side of the thing," he announced. "Of course, I do not intend to endorse any candidate."[8]

Graham aggressively tried to gain the support of the president of the United States in the Washington crusade. Truman brushed him off. Not only did he refuse to attend in person; he also refused even to endorse the rally. A White House memo reminded the evangelist and his team of the "show of himself" that Graham had made at the White House in 1950.

Reacting to his major snub by the president of the United States, Billy casually remarked to a reporter, "I guess he was just too busy or something." As if to react in kind to Truman's rejection of the evangelist, Graham later traveled to New York for a meeting with General Douglas MacArthur, who had suffered the ignominy of being fired by Harry Truman. "He is one of the most inspiring men I ever met," Billy gushed after meeting the general. "He is deeply religious."[9]

Despite his spectacular failure to enlist President Truman in the cause, Graham so successfully forged ties with governmental leaders in his Washington revival that he was even able to persuade Congress to allow a revival service outside the U.S. Capitol building. After all, declared Speaker of the House Sam Rayburn, the country needed a revival and Graham was the man to give it.

On February 3, 1952, Graham drew a Capitol crowd estimated by some longtime Washington reporters as bigger than most inauguration crowds. He gave the listeners the usual fare of hell and damnation, but he also laid out a specific five-point list of rules that America could adopt if it wished to preserve itself from destruction: (1) Maintain a strong military; (2) Maintain economic stability and security; (3) Continue to expose crime and irregularities in government; (4) Remain united by race, creed, age, and color; and (5) Foster a spiritual rejuvenation through individual faith in Christ, national humility, and united prayer.

Billy was not asking everyone who believed in Christ to accept one basic set of denominational beliefs. He was asking that the great numbers of worshippers, whatever their individual interpretation of scripture or their denominational affiliation, unite behind a general movement to place Christ first in their lives. It is surprising that none of the members of the House or Senate rushed Graham's bill of national particulars into law that very day.

By the end of the Washington crusade, Graham was telling reporters that a number of senators and members of the House of Representatives had suggested that he should run for the presidency at some time in his life. Although Billy emphasized that his evangelistic calling was paramount, he did say that if the country ever needed him to rescue it from communism he would serve the nation in any capacity.

PARTISAN POLITICS

Following the Washington crusade, oil industrialist Sid Richardson again urged Billy to make entreaties to General Eisenhower to run for president in 1952. Billy's taste for politics, especially after the Washington, D.C., crusade, was becoming more and more acute.

In late March, the evangelist flew to Paris to visit Eisenhower. The general shared personal stories about his early religious training. His parents had been in a church affiliated with the Mennonites and had studied the Bible with much devotion. His parents had taught him to memorize Scripture, just as Billy Graham's parents had taught the evangelist.

Graham encouraged the general to run for the presidency. Graham had now entered the world of American politics with a seriousness of purpose unlike any other evangelist before him. He had done it with much presumptuousness and also with the naive notion that it was all part of his religious calling, as if God were leading him to help select the Almighty's own candidate. Eisenhower gave no indications to Graham that he intended to run. Nevertheless, Graham left Paris convinced that he had just met the next president of the United States. He was right.

A NEW PRESIDENT AND CHRISTMAS AT THE FRONT

With the Korean War the dominant political issue, General Eisenhower rode his war celebrity into the 1952 campaign against Democratic candidate Adlai Stevenson of Illinois. While the general stayed above the political mudslinging, he dispatched his vice presidential candidate, Richard M. Nixon, to the front lines to hit the Democrats hard on the communist theme. Nixon accused Truman's secretary of state, Dean Acheson, of suffering color blindness toward the red menace, of not doing enough to root out those in government who would move the United States into the communist fold. Nixon even remarked that President Truman and his administration were "traitors to the high principles" that formed the nation.

Billy Graham joined in. His virulent anticommunism from the revival platform and his open remarks to many friends and associates about political issues and individuals made it clear to which party Graham was pledging his allegiance. Although he continued throughout his career to assert the non-partisan character of his revivals and his Christian message, Graham's politics never seemed far from the surface.

In Panmunjom, a South Korean village south of the 38th parallel, the peace talks between North and South Korea dragged on interminably while the casualties on both sides mounted. Following the election, President Eisenhower, who had promised to end the war, visited the troops before his inauguration. Nevertheless, the war continued through its third bitter and destructive winter, a brutal and deadly final period of slaughter that would continue for another six months.

During the Christmas season of 1952, Billy Graham accepted the pleas of numerous Army chaplains, missionaries, and others to visit the Korean War front. Accompanying Billy were Grady Wilson and Bob Pierce, an evangelist and journalist with Youth for Christ who would later found Samaritan's Purse, a charitable organization to care for the hungry and poor around the world. Ruth, who had attended high school in Korea, gave her blessing to the trip even though it meant Billy's separation from the family over the holiday season.

In a stopover in Japan, Graham met with General Mark Clark, commander of United Nations and United States troops in the Far East. Clark not only provided transportation and lodging for the Graham party's stay in Korea, but even helped, along with missionaries, to arrange for the individual appearances across the country. At a banquet in Tokyo before the flight to Korea, Graham addressed a gathering of 750 missionaries.

For two weeks, Graham traveled under military protection and supervision to towns and villages across Korea, meeting American soldiers and missionaries, visiting the wounded, and preaching the gospel on makeshift platforms near the front lines and in halls and schools in the larger communities. He held street meetings, visited hospitals for wounded children, and saw firsthand, for the first time in his life, the misery, hardship, and sorrow of war. In his diary, he speculated that the leaders who had bumbled and bungled their way into this conflict would some day have to answer to God Almighty. He talked about politicians selling the people down the river in secret agreements at so-called peace tables.

In the icy cold of the Korean winter, when temperatures sometimes fell to thirty degrees below zero, he preached sermons to groups of soldiers who had tears in their eyes that nearly froze. At one stop, he preached next to a painting depicting Christ watching over an exhausted soldier. The painting was done by one of the men in the audience.

He spent Christmas Eve of 1952 in a field hospital, going from bed to bed, trying to bring some comfort to the men far from home and their families and praying for God's healing. By the time he left the hospital that night, Billy said, he felt older and sadder but more aware of the needs of the suffering. As he returned from Korea to be united again with his family and the rest of his team, he was, he knew, a little wiser.

THE FAMILY AND THE TEAM

When William Franklin Graham III entered the world on July 14, 1952, Billy and Ruth's oldest daughter Gigi was seven years old, Anne was four, and Ruth (Bunny) was two. Billy said that he would have loved another girl but that every man needs a son.

Graham's career made extraordinary demands on his family. "The biggest event for the children," Ruth once said, "was when Daddy was home. They were mighty good about him being gone so much because they knew why he was gone."[10]

On one occasion, Ruth took Anne to one of the crusades to surprise Billy. When he first saw the four-year old, Ruth later recalled, Billy's face looked blank. He had not immediately recognized his own daughter.

Graham was not oblivious to the strain that his growing fame and its demands were causing to his relationship with his wife and children. However, his life was a mission from God, he believed, and he must follow it through. To Ruth he left an enormous challenge of balancing most of the family's responsibilities for child rearing with the demands of her public role—the wife and partner of one of the most recognized and revered public figures.

If Ruth Graham anchored the evangelist's life, his friends and professional associates—the now renowned Billy Graham team—kept the crusade machinery at full throttle. Maintenance of the organization took careful planning, tight organization, and focused and exemplary effort by talented individuals determined to stay the course.

The crusades of Billy Graham became like echoes of the Billy Sunday crusades—the advance workers and massive publicity, the cooperation of local churches and civic organizations, the big choirs, the call for converts. It is not surprising that the rallies of the Graham organization resembled those of Sunday.

Willis Haymaker, who had joined the Graham team at the South Carolina revival, constructed the organizational plan. He came with valuable first-hand experience at big-time American evangelism, having helped to organize campaigns not only for Billy Sunday but also for Gipsy Smith and others. Haymaker became the first official crusade director of the Billy Graham Evangelistic Association, directing the team in setting up the guidelines and procedures through which the BGEA staff selected sites and organized its evangelistic campaigns.

A revival started with an invitation. No plans for a Graham meeting would progress without a formal invitation, and the BGEA insisted that various ministerial associations and other Protestant religious and denominational bodies should join in it. The BGEA also encouraged politicians, college presidents, the media, industry leaders, and civic organizations to join. Such a coalition of forces requesting a revival in a city not only gave the meetings validity with the population, but it also vastly extended the revival's reach from the start. With this kind of ensured participation, the possibility that an individual revival would fail was greatly reduced.

As in the Sunday campaigns, the committee structure for Graham revivals was extensive. There were prayer committees, committees for men, women, children, counseling, prayer, follow-up, and assorted others.

A centrally located crusade office in the individual city operated from six months to a year prior to the start of the crusade so that as much of the work as possible could be completed before the meetings actually began.

The Graham team constantly emphasized to local communities that the purpose was not only to stimulate religious awakening in the community but also to encourage individuals to join and become part of regular church activities. A Graham crusade was intended, the team said, to make a permanent difference in the lives of the churches. Such a stance invariably gained increased participation and support by local pastors.

Perhaps the most sensitive of crusade functions, outside of the preaching of the evangelist, was that performed by the counselors. When Billy called for public commitments from individuals testifying that they had made a decision to turn their lives for Christ, the counselors stood ready to meet individually to confirm and clarify the decision. When convinced that the inquirer understood the meaning of the commitment to Jesus, the counselor noted on a card the nature of the decision. The convert then walked away with a copy of the Gospel of St. John and some Bible-study pamphlets. The card was then sent to the minister of the church of the individual's choice.

The permanent impact over the years on the lives of those who signed those decision cards pledging their lives to Christ has been difficult to assess. Surveys on the number who stayed connected to churches have varied. Some statistical studies indicate that the revivals did not significantly increase church rolls; others have pointed to a significant spiritual uplift in those cities that hosted rallies. The Graham organization has always maintained that their own follow-up work showed that well over half and as high as eighty percent of the lives of those who signed the cards were permanently affected in some way. For many of those who marched down the sawdust trail at Graham's calling, the decision was at least an affirmation of spiritual intent.

"You get a pat answer to all the nagging questions of modern living," says a former associate about Graham and his work, "and he's such an obviously nice guy. You go forward in the presence of thousands of others like you're wrapped in a massive security blanket. All you do is walk down the aisle and get eternal life. Where else can you get a bargain like that?"[11]

The organization was one thing; it took a capable team to put it all together. Billy Graham's team consisted of enormously gifted people who had been on promising career paths of their own. Each of them was willing to subordinate their egos for the good of the ministry. One key ingredient in Graham's success was that this core of men stood by him for over 40 years. He assembled the best evangelistic team of all time and they stayed together.

Usually working with Graham on the platform were soloist George Beverly Shea, who became Graham's radio partner in Chicago; choir director and master of ceremonies Cliff Barrows, whom Graham met in 1945; associate evangelist Grady Wilson, his boyhood friend; and pianist Tedd Smith, who hooked up with Billy at the Columbia, South Carolina, rally in 1951. This platform team—Graham, Barrows, Shea, Wilson, and Smith—was together at that South Carolina rally. When the Graham organization returned to Columbia 36 years later in 1987, the team was still together. When asked about former members of the team, one friend of Graham said, "If they're still alive they're still part of the team."[12]

NOTES

1. Vernon William Patterson, interview by Paul Erickson, (Collection 5, T4 Transcript), Archives of the Billy Graham Center, Wheaton College, Wheaton, Ill., 5 March 1985.

2. Busby, God's Ambassador, p. 58.

3. "Billy in Dixie," p. 55.

4. M. Miller, Plain Speaking, p. 363.

5. Galambos, Dwight David Eisenhower, pp. 696–97.

6. Graham, Just As I Am, p. 221.

7. Galambos, Dwight David Eisenhower, pp. 696–97.

8. The three quotes are all from "Rockin' the Capitol," Time, 3 March 1952, p. 76.

9. Ibid.

10. Busby, God's Ambassador, p. 67.

11. Fiske, "White House Chaplain."

12. "Billy Graham's Soulmate: Life Together."

Chapter 7

THE FIFTIES: THE MESSAGE AND THE MEDIA

ON COMMUNISTS AND CONSUMERS

To Billy Graham, the devil was not an abstraction but a literal force that had designed a ruthless system of political control that was sinking its claws in across the globe. You could see it in Russia and its buildup of nuclear weapons; you could see it in the unrest and ferment from the Orient to Latin America. The evil was communism. Billy saw the fight against communism as a battle to the death. Against this evil and its creator, the evangelist must pit all his strength and resolve and trust his ultimate weapon—the power of the Bible. Billy saw himself as God's instrument, a Christian soldier mobilizing for the greatest of all wars.

It was not at all complicated. On the one side was the towering evil; on the other, the army carrying the banner of fundamental biblical law. Billy believed he was fulfilling a divine mission, helping others find the way, to find the ultimate truths in their lives. America was losing its moral grip and sin was on the rampage. He was there to lead them all in a new direction.

"The Devil is their god; Marx, their prophet; Lenin their saint," Graham declared. Either communism must die "or Christianity must die, because it is actually a battle between Christ and anti-Christ"[1] It was a titanic struggle and America faced increasingly ominous times. "The forces of evil," said Billy, "are on the march."[2]

While attacking communism, Graham nevertheless held a grudging admiration for the passion it had inspired in many of its adherents. The communists demand from their followers everything, Graham said. In illustrating the undying commitment to the communist cause, he told the story of a young communist lieutenant, in charge of about 5,000 men, who came into a village in China, captured some missionaries, and then said that he was going to take another town about a mile away. When he was told that the other village had about 10,000 troops and that he and his men would die trying to take it, he said that he would gladly die to advance communism one-more mile.

It was this kind of motivation and discipline that made the communist threat so great. Its empire, Billy said, was about 800 million people and was penetrating every part of the world. It was challenging the Christian church as it had never been challenged before. Its disciples, like the lieutenant, were exercising self-denial, discipline, and dedication. They were willing to die for their beliefs or willing to go to prison. The devil had spirited warriors out to win the world.

These were the days of the junior senator from Wisconsin, Joseph McCarthy, who claimed to have lists of high-ranking public officials secretly allied with the Communist Party. These were the times when the media talked of the threat of nuclear weapons and the uncharted horrors that could lie ahead. Americans faced the postwar years with an increasing fear of Armageddon. They engaged in civil defense drills and built homemade bomb shelters. They watched the United States Congress interrogate Americans about their possible links to communist cells. They watched as writers and Hollywood personalities were paraded before inquisitors. They read in magazines and newspapers about the progress being made to devise new chemical and biological weapons. They read of the dire prospects of the world's population doubling before the end of the century and bringing poverty, disease, and new recruits for the communist regimes.

In a radio broadcast in 1953, Billy praised the investigations underway to root out communists: "While nobody likes a watchdog, and for that reason many investigation committees are unpopular, I thank God for men who, in the face of public denouncement and ridicule, go loyally on in their work of exposing the pinks, the lavenders and the reds who have sought refuge beneath the wings of the American eagle and from that vantage point try in every subtle, undercover way to bring comfort, aid and help to the greatest enemy we have ever known—communism."[3]

If most Americans were unable to describe exactly what communism was, they were still fearful of its threat. L. Nelson Bell, Graham's father-in-law, said that the purpose of communism was the "complete domination of the world" and that "America is in the gravest danger in her history."[4] Billy Graham himself compared the communist menace with the Revolutionary War and the Civil War as the greatest crises that America had ever faced.

If traitors were infiltrating the nation's highest offices, if communist leaders around the globe were arming against and aiming at the United States, where was the real protection for the average citizen? Billy Graham came to the rescue. He was there to offer protection for the trials that loomed. His shelter was the word of the gospel.

Despite mounting fear of global conflict, America in the 1950s was also entering an unprecedented consumer and technological dream world where new television sets and cars and automatic washing machines became staples for the average family. How could an individual living in one of the new, sprawling suburban communities, tinkering with his television test patterns on Saturday mornings and taking in a 25-cent show on Sundays, be an important part of overthrowing the menace of communism?

For followers of Billy Graham, the price in these schizophrenic times was not all that high. He did not ask them to give up their new suburban houses or their fast-food burgers or their Frigidares. He did chastise Americans for spending an inordinate amount of concern and energy over the frivolities of life, of caring more for their stock portfolios than their souls. He did refer to Americans as passengers on a sinking ship making their own cabins more comfortable. He did talk about how coveting had become a great sin in America that was sapping the country's energy. However, he never said that they had to give it all up. Indeed, Graham even closed a sermon once with the line, "God bless you and thank you, and God bless the Holiday Inns."[5]

The sacrifice, the commitment, was personal salvation alone. Merely by Americans having faith in God, by rejecting sin and living decent lives, all the communist menace could be wiped away. It was that simple. The soldiers in the Christian army did not have to wear fatigues; they could wear suits and drive Buicks.

Anticommunism helped make Billy Graham into a national figure. His encouragement of a return to religion had a two-edged purpose. In addition to the intrinsic value of personal faith in God, Graham declared that religion itself was the weapon with which communism could be defeated. Graham told the faithful that they were perfect creations of God. Despite mounting fears, listeners felt a greater sense of worth when they listened to Graham. If communism was infecting millions of individuals around the globe, it could not touch them if Christ was in their hearts. Through a religious revival, a turning back to old-fashioned Christian ideals and Americanism, the communist threat could be thwarted. After all, the President of the United States, Dwight D. Eisenhower, declared that "it is only through religion that we can lick this thing called communism."[6]

It was no coincidence that on July 11, 1955, President Dwight D. Eisenhower signed Public Law 140 making it mandatory that all coinage and paper currency display the motto "In God We Trust." The following year, Public Law 851 was enacted by Congress, supported by both political parties and all political persuasions. It officially replaced the national motto, "E Pluribus Unum," with "In God We Trust," the motto that had been introduced at the time of the country's founding. All of this activity at the height of cold war tension was an effort to portray the division between Judeo-Christian civilization and the "godless" menace of communism. Indeed, the new national motto was only part of a broader effort to bring greater religious presence in civic ritual and symbols. On June 14, 1954, Congress unanimously ordered the inclusion of the words "Under God" into the nation's Pledge of Allegiance.

Billy Graham was welcomed in the fifties not only because of his growing image as the religious spokesman railing against evil but also because he epitomized the fifties. In appearance and style, in his emphasis on the family, and in his message of thrift, hard work, and the reality of the American dream, he personified those qualities that Americans trusted. Whether listening to him on the radio, watching him on television, or attending a rally, many began to see Graham as something of a national counselor.

He told them to set a parental example, to keep families together with the husband as the head of the house and the wife at home with the children. He even told women to be attractive for their husbands, to keep a clean house, and to refrain from nagging and complaining. Every wife had the right to expect husbands to be loving, gentle, and polite, but every husband had the right to expect a wife to adapt to "his interests, his experience, his progress... in the evening, run out and meet him and give him a kiss. Give him love at any cost."[7] The solution, then, to all problems great and not so great, from the Bomb to diaper changing, was simple, evangelical, and socially conservative.

He spoke often about the prosperity of America, about the nation having the highest standard of living in the world, and about the tremendous educational advantages Americans enjoyed. In spite of this good fortune, however, something was wrong. He quoted a psychiatrist who claimed that ninety percent of American homes were unhappy. He talked about youthful licentiousness, alcoholism, and the lure of a new music beginning to sweep the nation called rock and roll. "Pajama parties, sex orgies, drunken parties, running with gangs were all part of the teenagers' search for God...sex is something you were built for, but it was made to be controlled...if you lose the sex battle you have lost the battle of life."[8]

He talked about soaring divorce rates and rising crime. He quoted the director of the Federal Bureau of Investigation, J. Edgar Hoover, who warned that the nation was facing such a crime epidemic that it could lead to national ruin.

Once again, the answer was the same. America had strayed from its Christian roots. To be a true American patriot was to accept Christ. If President Truman had declared that the world stood on the very "edge of Hell," it was up to individuals to make a complete about-face from that precipice. He was reaffirming the ideals and values that he believed had given meaning and order to American life.

In this 1950s Cold War atmosphere, it was not difficult for Graham to equate patriotism, loyalty, and the quest for happiness with a Christian ideal. The response to threats abroad and turmoil in American society, from youthful rebellion to a decline in moral values, was an awakening of religious impulses. It was, he said, not that the country was losing its reason, but that it was losing its hope. It had become soft and flabby in its beliefs and vulnerable as never before. To regain the spirit of the pioneer and the zest for life was the great challenge.

When Graham opened his crusade in Melbourne, Australia, in April 1959, the film On the Beach was being shot. The film, based on the bestselling book by Nevil Shute, was set in 1964, five years in the future. A nuclear war, precipitated by a small, unnamed country, creates a ghastly radioactive cloud that is slowly enveloping the planet and destroying all human life. When the movie opens, all human beings in the Northern Hemisphere have perished. The southern half of the world has only four more months before it too succumbs to the poisoning. Melbourne, at the southern end of the continent, will survive the longest, but for the people there, it's also just a matter of time.

The filming of On the Beach was a remarkable backdrop to the Billy Graham crusade in Australia. "As we look at problems...facing mankind today," he declared, "we see that this is an age of confusion and frustration, fear and anxiety, hopelessness and almost despair."[9]

The movie being shot, he said, reflected the pessimism that was rampant worldwide. For his listeners in Australia as well as those in the United States and around the globe, it was a matter of devoting one's life to God.

Billy Graham saw God as so intimately involved in his own life and the lives of others that everyday occurrences such as the weather were revealing either of God's favor or his unhappiness. He also saw the devil as an active force. When the evangelist suffered a kidney stone that almost prevented his preaching, he speculated that the devil might be mounting a vengeful attack against him. Prayer, he believed, could persuade God to cure illness. What about the many times faithful Christians did not have their illnesses cured through prayer? In many cases, Billy believed, God's wishes and ways were beyond human understanding.

Much of his own personal life, he believed, was evidence either of God's approval or scolding. He fervently believed that God was so closely involved in his personal affairs that such decisions as his education, his marriage, his trips, even his routines had been influenced by the Almighty. He lived an almost obsessive existence, trying to determine God's wishes or directions to follow. Did God mean for him to begin this particular crusade at this time? Did God mean for him to take a few days off to recover after a crusade? Was this illness or that some kind of divine retribution?

He knew in his mind that he was carrying God's word to the world. It was his responsibility to discern even the minutest divine direction. He knew always that his main job was persuading the masses to try as hard as he did to identify God's wishes and plans. If he could achieve this lofty ambition, all manner of evil could be wiped away, from the hydrogen bomb to kidney stones.

A FLEDGLING MEDIA STAR

Billy Graham was in many ways a product of America's new mass culture, an emblem of the times, competing in the market place with political figures, entertainers, and sports figures. His style and personality, his allegiance to individualism, and his faith in American ways made him a marketer's dream. He was a phenomenon of the mass media. He was, in short, a star.

He often denied it. He claimed that the masses came to his revivals not to see him and the spectacle he brought with him but to hear and respond to the message. This was not entertainment, he said. Nevertheless, like crowds in the fifties gathered to hear such star attractions as Elvis Presley, Billy Graham admirers sometimes gathered at events more than three hours before he was due to arrive. At one Sydney, Australia, meeting in 1959, fans greeted Graham as he left the plane with a deafening cheer; they waved hats and handkerchiefs and broke into song.

Watching television was only recently becoming a national pastime in Australia, and the Australian Broadcasting Network had aired a number of features about Graham prior to the visit. At the meeting itself, more than 500 people, mostly teenagers, screamed as he walked to the dais and pressed against a rope fence to take pictures and ask for autographs. Twenty ushers tried vainly to keep the crowd back as teenage girls pushed forward to try to touch Graham.

At another crusade, a reporter asked several questions about the operation of the Billy Graham organization and its finances and whether Graham himself expected to make substantial money. As the reporter continued to press Graham, Billy reached inside his coat pocket for a telegram he had received earlier that day. If he were interested in making money, Billy said, grinning, he would take advantage of an offer like this. The telegram was from a Hollywood company that wanted Graham to star in two motion pictures, offering him a substantial amount of money.

Billy would not become an actor. Nevertheless, a *Woman's Day* article called him a star evangelist and reported that he was beginning to use all the gimmicks of a film studio to boost his celebrity. He also began to use all the power of the emerging mass media.

In January 1921, station KDKA in Pittsburgh had carried the first church service live on the radio. In the years following, Americans tuned in on their new radio sets, and infant commercial stations hurried to the airwaves. In 1922 Paul Radar, pastor of the Chicago Gospel Tabernacle, set up his own once-a-week station with the call letters WJBT ("Where Jesus Blesses Thousands"). Rader and his team broadcast all day on Sundays and later negotiated a network deal for a full hour each weekday.

From the Moody Bible Institute in Chicago to small stations in St. Louis, Denver, Cincinnati, and Richmond, Virginia, radio religious pioneers stepped to the microphone for Christ. From the sanctuary of Calvary Church of Placentia, California, Charles Fuller launched a radio ministry in 1925 that evolved into the *Old-Fashioned Revival Hour*. By 1939, *Old-Fashioned Revival Hour* reached approximately 10 million listeners. At the time of Fuller's death in 1968, the broadcast aired to more than 500 stations around the world.

In October 1930, CBS launched Walter Maier's *The Lutheran Hour*, from the studios of WHK in Cleveland. With most of the subsequent broadcasts originating from KFUO in St. Louis, the show succeeded beyond Maier's wildest dreams. By 1935, CBS estimated that *The Lutheran Hour* reached an average of several million listeners in each broadcast. Maier's team lived up to the show's motto—to "Bring Christ to the Nations." *The Lutheran Hour* continues to this day.

Of all the early Christian radio broadcasters, it was Walter Maier that Billy Graham most admired. When Billy was at Western Springs and first hosted his weekly program *Songs in the Night* at the tiny WCFL station in Chicago, the unknown young evangelist invited Maier, a widely respected Christian radio celebrity, to make an appearance. Surprisingly, Maier complied. Billy never forgot the interest that Maier had taken in the struggling minister at that time in his life.

Shortly after Billy Graham's triumph in the Los Angeles crusade and during the Boston crusade in 1950, Walter Maier was critically ill in the hospital. His son, Paul Maier, remembered Billy Graham making special efforts to contact Maier: "And one of the telegrams read, '15,000 Christians gathered in prayer for your recovery. Signed, Billy Graham.' And I recall asking my mother who this was and then she supplied some of the detail, and I held one of the telegrams up to my father in the oxygen tent, and he smiled, knowing him, and shook his head, knowing who he was, and thrilled indeed, I suppose, in his last moments, that...that Dr. Graham knew he was ill and was praying for him, which I think is a kind of a perfect passing of the torch as it were, my father just dying, and then Dr. Graham coming to very sudden prominence after that."[10]

Later in 1950, Billy and Cliff Barrows attended a religious conference in Ocean City, New Jersey. Also at the conference was Theodore Elsner, the president of National Religious Broadcasters. Elsner and the religious broadcasting industry had been rocked by the sudden death that summer of Walter Maier. Who would replace him? Elsner, who knew of Graham's growing fame and oratorical presence, thought he knew the answer. Billy was unsure.

Elsner persisted. He approached several businessmen in the industry, persuaded the American Broadcasting Company that Graham should be the man, and arranged for subsequent meetings with the evangelist. Billy resisted. He did not think he had the time to mix a radio ministry with his crusade schedule, he said, or the money necessary to launch a radio enterprise. At a Portland, Oregon, crusade in the summer of 1950, Billy met with associates in a hotel room, led them in prayer, and finally agreed. Even then, he wanted a certain sign that it was God's will. He would make an announcement, he said, for donations at the next crusade meeting. If the contributions reached $25,000 by midnight he would agree; a penny less and he would not do it.

On the night he chose to deliver the message about the possible radio commitment, lines of contributors stuffed bills, coins, and pledges, scribbled on programs and song sheets, into a shoebox. The contribution totaled less than $25,000. Graham took that as a sign that he should not do it. Starting the radio program with less than the full amount might be a trap set by Satan.

When the evangelist and his discouraged troops reached the hotel, Grady Wilson thought to pick up some letters that had been left at the hotel desk. When Billy opened each of them, there were checks with the specific instruction that they be used for a radio broadcast ministry. The contributions in the letters put the amount over the top. Graham thought it was a miracle.

During the discussions surrounding Billy Graham's new radio show, Ruth Graham suggested the name. On November 5, 1950, the first weekly broadcast of *The Hour of Decision,* featuring Billy Graham, originated from the site of the Atlanta crusade, the Ponce de Leon baseball stadium. One hundred and fifty ABC affiliate stations carried it. Following the sermon, he closed with a benediction that would be heard on subsequent broadcasts year after year: "And now, until next week, goodbye and may the Lord bless you, real good [sic]!"

Within a matter of weeks, *The Hour of Decision* surpassed the previous all-time high for a religious broadcast with more than 20 million listeners. Within 20 years, the show would be carried on over 1,200 stations nationwide.

From the earliest broadcasts, Billy encouraged listeners to write letters. In the first year alone, nearly 200,000 letters arrived at the BGEA headquarters. As Billy suggested in the broadcasts, all the writers had to do was address the envelope to "Billy Graham, Minneapolis, Minnesota."

Billy Graham saw clearly the tremendous potential of radio and also the newer medium—television. He had entered the realm of what was already transforming the face of society in the fifties. The popularity of *The Hour of Decision* soon convinced the BGEA that Graham should air portions of the show on television. Some programs featured filmed segments from the live crusades, where the immense crowds and Billy's oratory provided a glimpse to many viewers of what it might be like to attend one of the crusades in person. Those first telecasts featured Cliff Barrows leading a huge chorus in familiar hymns, George Beverly Shea singing "How Great Thou Art," a celebrity giving a testimony to the saving power of the Lord, part of Graham's sermon, and shots of people streaming to the front to make their decisions for Christ. Graham made a few adjustments to his speaking style so that the cameramen would have less difficulty in maneuvering his image on the small screen. The basic elements of the broadcasts were usually the highlights of crusades.

Billy also produced some segments in a living-room or study setting discussing events of the day and the power of the gospel to change the country's direction and the course of individual lives. After running for nearly three years with a very modest viewing audience, Graham and his advisors temporarily gave up the television experiment, at least for a while. There were other media to try.

Billy Graham Evangelistic Films, later called World Wide Pictures, began to release out of its office and studios in Burbank, California, a series of films, both documentary and dramatic, that sponsors of crusades used for instruction. One of the films, *His Eye Is on the Sparrow*, starred the black singer and actress Ethel Waters, who became involved in the Billy Graham crusades after her personal life was profoundly changed by attending one of the rallies.

Graham later told the story of waking up in the middle of a night in 1953 with the idea of founding a magazine. He walked over to his desk and wrote down ideas about its content, contributors, and other aspects of the publication. The next morning he shared the idea with Ruth and they prayed together about whether to go forward. After consulting with Ruth's father, who had founded a magazine called the *Presbyterian Journal*, they decided that the new publication would give evangelical writers and thinkers a forum that they currently lacked.

Within three years, with the help of conservative Christian scholar Carl F. H. Henry, a former professor at Fuller Theological Seminary, Graham had founded a magazine called *Christianity Today*. Aimed at an audience of ministers and religious students, it would become the most highly visible and respected publication in the United States reflecting theological perspectives of evangelicals about American life and politics. Not surprisingly, the publication was staunchly free-market and loudly virulent on the issue of communism and its atheistic roots.

It would be the 1957 crusade in Madison Square Garden that would mark a momentous leap forward in Graham's use of television. His ministry, however, was already of the nation. Through the media, people in cities and small towns in every state in the country now understood what Billy Graham was all about.

NOTES

1. Frady, *American Righteousness*, p. 237.

2. Graham sermon, Charlotte campaign file, Archives of the Billy Graham Center, Wheaton College, Wheaton, Ill., 24 September 1958.

3. Bloom, "The Preacher: Billy Graham."

4. Bell, "A Layman and His Faith," p. 19.

5. Frady, *American Righteousness*, p. 237.

6. "President Sees Editors," *New York Times*, 10 April 1953.

7. Martin, *Prophet with Honor*, p. 159.

8. Judith Smart, "The Evangelist as Star: The Billy Graham Crusade in Australia, 1959," *Journal of Popular Culture*, summer (1999): 165.

9. L. Nelson Bell, *Sydney Morning Herald*, 13 April 1959.

10. Paul Maier, interview by Robert Shuster, (CN 49, #T1), Archives of the Billy Graham Center, Wheaton College, Wheaton, Ill., 9 November 1978.

Chapter 8

THE LONDON
CRUSADE OF 1954

When Billy Graham first set foot on British ground as a member of Youth for Christ in 1946, he had a keen sense that this was a special place in his life. In the war-torn cities and towns of Great Britain, he had felt an unusual kinship with the people, a respect for the trials they had endured, and a feeling that he could make a difference in many of their lives. Along with Cliff Barrows, he had returned to Britain months later. This journey was one he would repeat again and again.

In 1954, after he had made news across the Atlantic with his revival successes and increasing media attention, Billy accepted an invitation from a group of evangelical leaders to hold a full-scale, three-month crusade in London. Despite his enthusiasm for undertaking the revival, Graham knew that it would present greater challenges than any he had ever faced.

Preparations for such a major revival in Europe would be daunting. The logistics of travel, publicity, and local arrangements would take extraordinary teamwork, coordination, and a dedicated group of both American and British workers.

Evangelical churches in Great Britain represented only a fraction of the population they did in the United States, both in total numbers and as a percentage of the total Christian community. An invitation to Graham from the small evangelical groups in Great Britain was one thing; a welcome from other religious communities was another.

Many church leaders felt Graham's message to be simplistic, a warmed-over theology that ignored recent Biblical scholarship. They feared a negative reaction among their own congregations from the circus-like trappings that such a spectacle would present. They resented an upstart American evangelist with his "hot-gospel" salesman pitch.

The British press was especially hostile to the planned revival. Many columnists hurled invective and insults, questioned Graham's motives, accused him of seeking a fortune rather than souls, and mocked his presumptuous quest to travel the Atlantic to tell the British people how to live their lives.

Graham alternated between determination and anxiety. He asked Ruth to accompany him, although that would mean leaving the four children with family and friends for an extended period of time. She agreed on the condition that she could return home after the first month.

Graham prepared for the London crusade as if he were going into battle. He contacted the numerous individuals he had met through the Youth for Christ rallies in Britain to enlist their support. Convinced that a massive publicity drive was necessary to ensure that knowledge of his meetings penetrated the usual London swirl of advertising, he organized his own blitz to dwarf other entertainment mediums vying for attention. The team produced 10,000 press announcements, 30,000 posters, and advertisements on the sides of buses bearing the simple message "Hear Billy Graham!" The budget for spreading the message exceeded $50,000.

The team enlisted 18,000 people in England to participate in prayer rallies even before the evangelist had left the American continent. Graham met with President Eisenhower, who wished him well, and managed to convince Secretary of State John Foster Dulles to write letters to diplomatic contacts and to issue a statement declaring, in the most diplomatic terms possible, that Britain could use a spiritual renaissance. Winthrop Aldrich, the American Ambassador to Great Britain, also promised to lend assistance. Two U.S. senators, Stuart Symington of Missouri and Styles Bridges of New Hampshire, agreed to make the trip with Graham, giving the whole enterprise an aura of a diplomatic as well as a religious mission.

In February 1954, the Graham team embarked for Great Britain by ship. Graham became increasingly fearful that Londoners might spitefully reject this young American minister's crusade as an affront to their own national identity. Already the press was on the attack. Shortly before the arrival of the *S.S. United States* in Southampton, an editorial writer for the *London Evening News* lambasted Billy as nothing more than an actor/manager of a show who strolls his listeners "down Pavements of Gold, introduces them to a rippling-muscled Christ who resembles Charles Atlas [a famous bodybuilder] with a halo, then drops them abruptly into the Lake of Fire for a simple scalding."[1]

Another reporter declared in earshot of Grady Wilson that when Jesus was on Earth he did not travel by luxurious ocean liner, as Billy Graham had. Grady yelled out, "Listen man, if you can find me a donkey that can swim the Atlantic, I'll buy it on the spot."[2]

Graham's first days in London were tense. The team had envisioned in the planning stages of the crusade that the revival would take place in a futuristic, aluminum tabernacle constructed with a series of concentric rings that could be raised and lowered. This would be a Graham innovation, appropriate for a revival as important as that being planned for London. After consultations with scientists and architects and some artist's renderings, the planners decided the contraption would not work. Thus, the crusade's organizers were forced at the last minute to look for a satisfactory venue in the London area that could hold thousands of people on consecutive days for three months. They settled for the Harringay Arena, located in a drab section of North London, a place most notable for its boxing matches, hockey games, and circuses. It was located next to a dog track. Understandably, the revival planners were nervous that many Londoners would be reluctant to attend religious rallies in such a setting.

On the opening night, with a freezing drizzle casting an ominous gloom over London, Graham called to the arena from his hotel near Oxford Circus to ask an assistant about the size of the gathering crowd. He was disappointed by the response. Few had yet arrived. Characteristically pessimistic, Graham imagined a hall filled with few worshippers but with an army of reporters ready to mock him and his crusade, to make him a laughingstock. Battling a cold and with it a hoarseness that threatened to dull his oratorical power, he at one point fell to his knees in prayer.

As Billy and Ruth rode by taxi through the darkness, with the sleet splashing the windshield, they felt near remorse over the dire prospects. Yet, when they arrived, one of Graham's team rushed up to meet them and announced that the arena was jammed with people.

All of the worry and anxiety were washed away in a sea of faces as Graham strode into the arena and mounted the platform with the crowd already joining in a rousing hymn. Nearly 15,000 people had crowded a facility built to hold 11,500. It was a remarkable outpouring of support for the 35-year-old American preacher from North Carolina.

In full voice, Graham spoke on the topic "Does God Matter?" The giant throng in the audience had already given Billy the answer he wished to hear.

Following his sermon and the invitation to come down the aisle, nearly 200 responded. One member of the audience later remembered how unusual was the sound, in the quiet of the hall, of shoes creaking on the wood floor as the worshippers came forward.

The crowds had responded and they continued to respond. The rain and sleet of the first night in London turned to snow the next day and yet the crowd did not diminish. Harringay had a reputation of not drawing full houses in consecutive evenings for any speaker. Graham shattered that barrier. Even on a March evening in which snow fell in London, Harringay sheltered more than 10,000.

Maurice Rowlandson, one of the organizers of the London revival, remembered his amazement at the crowds he saw night after night and the stories he heard from those who had marched down the aisle in answer to Graham's call. Most were ordinary people, he said, but others included heralded names such as Ernest Shippen, a prominent London businessman and producer of Shippen's Meat paste, a cracker spread that graced tea time tables of thousands of British citizens. Shippen, said Rowlandson, was an alcoholic and his terrible temper had forced his wife and family to live in fear. "He was one of those who responded and both his life and the life of his family was totally changed from then on."[3]

As the crusade moved into April, crowds were daily jamming into the arena well before the scheduled start. Graham was drawing socialites as well as average workers, along with an increasing number of British clerics. Even the established clergy, most of whom had scorned Graham when he first arrived, now began to acknowledge that the British people had responded in astonishingly powerful ways to Graham and his message.

The British Broadcasting Company asked him to speak on radio. European television and radio stations carried film clips of the meetings. The press, which had built up a crescendo of opposition, now became less hostile. When one reporter in the London Daily Express wrote an article full of effusive praise for the evangelist, Graham realized the impact that the crusade had already made.

With the revival exceeding even the most grandiose of expectations, Graham's organizing committee decided to unleash the available technology to reach beyond London. The team negotiated to have 400 telephone-type message lines to transmit the revival services to loudspeakers set up in halls, arenas, cinemas, churches, and other locations all across England, Scotland, Ireland, and Wales. Hosted by local clergymen or town officials, the gatherings included singing, prayers, and other preliminaries before the Graham sermon. The London crusade was thus becoming a British campaign without Graham leaving the Harringay location.

As the crusade continued, the intense pressure and non-stop activity were beginning to take a toll on the evangelist. Graham lost weight from his already reed-thin frame. He began to appear haggard at times and dark lines surrounded his eyes. Nevertheless, he continued at a frantic pace, convinced that the Lord had blessed the London revival and determined that he was not about to let down the Lord.

Ruth displayed extraordinary stamina. On many nights, long after Graham had left the arena, she stayed to counsel worshippers. On one night she consoled a woman whose husband had died only a week before. Ruth later told Billy that she had felt totally inadequate to help the woman in her great emotional pain and distress. Twelve years later, Ruth received a letter from the woman who credited the Harringay crusade and Ruth's help with turning her life around. She had joined a singing group with the Salvation Army.

Although Londoners marveled at the religious sensation of the events at Harringay, British theologians, along with the public, disagreed, sometimes vehemently, about whether the Graham crusade would have any lasting spiritual benefit. Although Graham was a commanding presence on stage, was his impact more akin to that of a political orator or an entertainer than that of a man infused with the spirit of God, instilling a genuine spirit of conversion among those assembled in the giant arena? Would their lives be permanently altered by the event or would the occasion be remembered mostly as a community happening? Was this crusade evidence of God working through the evangelist or was it an ego-driven, publicity-seeking performer having his time in the sun at the expense of British society?

The debate continued but Graham continued to amass large crowds. At Trafalgar Square, London's most famous outdoor square, Graham conducted an open-air service in early April that scattered the hundreds of pigeons that normally take over much of the area and drew over 10,000 onlookers, the largest gathering at that historic central London site since a celebration honoring soldiers at the end of World War II.

Graham held a rally at another of London's historic sites—Hyde Park. For over three centuries, Londoners had gathered at Hyde Park to witness everything from horseracing to political protest. On Good Friday of 1954, an estimated 50,000 onlookers gathered to hear America's famous evangelist.

Graham himself remained a model of humble bearing, crediting the human outpouring to God's work, remaining gracious in the face of ostracism and parody, and ascribing honest motives to those who doubted the religious conviction of the crusade or the theology behind it.

Graham confronted one of his most persistent and acerbic critics, William Conner of London's *Daily Mirror*, by repeatedly asking him for a meeting. Conner, who wrote a column in the newspaper under the pseudonym "Cassandra," finally agreed to meet with Graham under the condition that the evangelist would join him in a pub called The Baptist's Head, not a usual meeting place to discuss religion but a place sporting a name that could not have been more appropriate.

Cordiality reigned at The Baptist's Head. Conner and Graham got along famously, the tough reporter and the preacher, a teetotaler. Although Graham did not convince his journalistic nemesis of his theology, he did convince him of his sincerity. "I never thought that simplicity could cudgel us sinners so hard," Cassandra wrote, "We live and learn— the bloke means everything he says."[4]

The London crusade gave life to one of the most popular hymns of praise. Although the American singer James Caldwell had introduced "How Great Thou Art" at a bible conference on Long Island in 1951, it was not until George Beverly Shea and Cliff Barrows used it extensively in London that the hymn gained its enormous popularity. Derived from an original Swedish poem entitled "O Sotre Gud," (O Mighty God) written by Swedish churchman Carl Boborg in 1886, "How Great Thou Art" is now familiar to believers and nonbelievers alike across the world. Its power echoes from the days at Harringay.

When the Graham team members had planned the London crusade, they had reserved Harringay for 12 weeks, expecting the meetings to last no longer than 6 weeks. Not only had the crowds continued to pack the arena; Graham had filled halls and other venues around greater London on several occasions. He decided to continue the revival through the full 12 weeks, despite the fact that he, along with the entire team, was completely fatigued. They decided to hold the last two services not at Harringay but at the two largest stadiums in London—White City and Wembley. Both were available for May 22, 1954. The Graham team had engineered a triumphal end to what had been an extraordinary religious revival.

On May 22, Graham drew an estimated 65,000 at White City Stadium. After the service, as the team prepared to travel to Wembley for the late afternoon rally, Graham was told that crowds were snarling traffic. Perhaps a helicopter could be arranged. Instead, the London police arranged a special escort for the team bus.

As Graham arrived at Wembley, the gates had already been closed. The crowd had engulfed every inch of the famous stadium, including the soccer field. With a stinging sleet pelting the crowd, tens of thousands of raised black umbrellas gave the scene something of an otherworldly cast. With many royal visitors as well as government leaders in attendance, Graham had been tempted to insert a greater amount of intellectual content in his prepared sermon. He resisted this impulse, deciding that he would appear phony. He would go with his usual simple, direct call for redemption. The sermon was called "Choose This Day Whom You Will Serve."

Despite the frigid, numbing rain, no one left Wembley Stadium. Graham later said that he felt that the singing and the fellowship, there in the cold rain, had somehow bonded the thousands, "all of us together, shoulders hunched against the elements, squinting through the torrents, listening to the music. Bev sang, and I prayed in utter simplicity."[5] He was grateful, he said, that he had not succumbed to the temptation to be something he was not.

Several thousand people sloshed through the water and mud to the platform when Graham issued his invitation to come forward. The Archbishop of Canterbury, Geoffrey Fisher, the spiritual leader of the Church of England whose role extended to the sponsorship of interfaith relations in the country, was a prominent participant. The Archbishop later told Grady Wilson that they might never again, this side of heaven, see a sight such as they had just witnessed.

On that day alone, Billy Graham had preached in person to approximately 200,000. Over the three-month period, more than 2 million people in Great Britain had seen or listened to Graham. More than 38,000 had marched down the sawdust trail.

On the morning of Graham's scheduled departure from London, he got a totally unexpected telephone call from one of the personal secretaries of Prime Minister Winston Churchill. The secretary said that the Prime Minister would like to meet with Graham the following day. Exhausted, packing his bags, Graham hastily answered that a meeting would be impossible because of prior plans to leave by train that evening. After the phone call, Graham was aghast at his own action, realizing that he had just turned down Winston Churchill, the leader who had guided the allies through their darkest hours of World War II. However, after a few moments, the phone rang again. The secretary asked if Billy could meet Churchill at noon. "I dressed," Billy wrote later, "and shot over to 10 Downing Street."[6]

As he walked into the dimly lit room, Billy saw at the end of the conference table the short, balding, legendary figure whose face was known throughout the world. Not surprisingly, he was holding a cigar. To Billy, he seemed pensive. He asked the evangelist what hope he held out for the world.

Graham pulled out a copy of the New Testament from his pocket and told Churchill that he was filled with hope. Astonishingly, the excited Graham began to sermonize about the significance of Jesus on the cross and his own earnest belief that the Lord would come again to draw a glorious curtain on human history. Churchill listened closely, telling the evangelist that he agreed with the substance of his remarks and that only a return to God could bring hope for the future. The conversation lasted about 40 minutes, far longer than had been scheduled or than either Graham or Churchill had expected. When he looked back on the meeting years later, Graham said he felt that speaking with Winston Churchill was almost like conferring with a part of history.

The Harringay crusade had given the career of Billy Graham an enormous jolt of publicity. His impact on London in those weeks had been remarkable. Even diplomatic officials in Washington said that the Graham revival had brought the two countries closer together.

The revival energized the lives of young evangelical students. Several years after the crusade, it was clear that the number of evangelical pastors had increased dramatically in Great Britain. Many of those individuals credited the crusade with infusing their lives with purpose and determination.

David Frost, the internationally known television interviewer and talk show host, remembered seeing Billy Graham at Harringay in 1954, that "amazing crusade starting with the vilification from all the press and ending up with the press on his side and the Archbishop of Canterbury doing the prayers or whatever at Wembley Stadium."[7]

Along with Frost, hundreds of thousands, for a few weeks in 1954, had turned a drab north London prizefight arena into a phenomenon. At this stage of Graham's career, it had been his greatest triumph.

NOTES

1. Wacker, "Charles Atlas with a Halo," pp. 336–41.
2. Busby, God's Ambassador, p. 74.
3. Rowlandson, "50 Years in Christian Work."
4. Martin, Prophet with Honor, p. 182.
5. Graham, Just As I Am, p. 274.
6. Busby, God's Ambassador, p. 82.
7. "A Talk Show Legend," Challenge Online, issue 6, 18 February 2002, http://www.challengeweekly.co.nz/Iss06–2002.htm.

Billy Graham, approximately 6 months old, with his mother. Courtesy of the Billy Graham Evangelical Association.

Billy Graham as a teen. Courtesy of the Billy Graham Evangelical Association.

Billy and Ruth Graham at Wheaton College. Courtesy of the Billy Graham Evangelical Association.

The Frank Graham family. Back row, left to right: Catherine, Billy, Melvin, Jean. Seated: Morrow and Frank. Courtesy of the Billy Graham Evangelical Association.

Graham shakes hands with a prisoner at Bridewell, the county jail in Chicago, Illinois, June 1, 1962. Graham addressed the audience of 1,700 prisoners on his visit as part of a 19-day crusade in Chicago. (AP/WIDE WORLD Photos)

Billy Graham poses with his wife, Ruth, and their three daughters on the liner Queen Mary *following his arrival in New York City on July 7, 1954. The daughters are, Ruth, 3, in front, Anne, 6, left, and Virginia, 8. (AP/WIDE WORLD Photos)*

In his youth, Billy Graham dreamed of becoming a major league baseball player. Although he would make his mark in another field of endeavor, Graham appeared often in sports stadiums. In June 1960, at Griffith Stadium in Washington, D.C., the evangelist delivers a stirring message. The Library of Congress, LC-U9-4619 (05).

The Graham family, 1962. Left to right: Franklin, Ned, Ruth, Billy and (Bunny) Ruth. Back row: Anne and Gigi. Courtesy of the Billy Graham Evangelical Association.

In May 1970, at the height of the protests against the Vietnam War and shortly after students had been killed by National Guard troops at Kent State University, President Richard Nixon decided to attend a Billy Graham rally at the University of Tennessee's Neyland Stadium. Because of the timing of the visit and its overtly political nature, Nixon's appearance sparked angry demonstrations. National Archives and Records Administration, Nixon Presidential Materials, NS-WHPO: White House Photo Office Collection, NLNP-WHPO-MPF-C3587(04).

Evangelist Billy Graham, center, is joined by North Carolina Gov. Mike Easley, left, and Graham's son Franklin Graham, right, during the groundbreaking ceremony for the new headquarters for the Billy Graham Evangelistic Association in Charlotte, N.C., Tuesday, Oct. 29, 2002. Shown in background is Charlotte mayor Pat McCrory. (AP/ WIDE WORLD Photos)

Chapter 9

THE GRAHAM
PHENOMENON IN NEW YORK

The London crusade had established the Billy Graham revival team as a burgeoning force in big-time evangelism. Photographs of Graham preaching from the Harringay arena and the immense crowds of Londoners who gathered there to hear him appeared in newspapers across Europe. Suddenly Graham was in great demand in cities that he barely knew existed.

Although surprised by the growing international attention, the evangelist did not wilt under its avalanche of publicity and the invitations to begin new crusades. In Stockholm, Sweden, and Copenhagen, Denmark, Graham drew the same kinds of immense throngs that had gathered in London. In Berlin, Germany, he preached at the same stadium where a young American black athlete, Jesse Owens, had won four gold medals in the 1936 Olympics in front of a crowd that included Nazi leader Adolf Hitler.

Graham also returned to Great Britain, where he conducted a six-week stand in Glasgow, Scotland, and a weeklong series of meetings at London's Wembley Stadium, where he had preached a year earlier. While in Great Britain, Graham was invited to preach on Easter Sunday to Queen Elizabeth, the Duke of Edinburgh, and other members of the royal family in the chapel at Windsor Castle.

When Graham walked into the chapel, he realized that it had no pulpit. He had carried with him a sheaf of handwritten notes as he usually had done for his sermons. This time he would have to speak without them. Although he later remembered feeling his heart pounding furiously at the prospect, he managed to get through the presentation unscathed.

In January and February 1956, Graham ventured from Europe into the Far East with a tour of India. Before leaving the United States, the evangelist received a call from Secretary of State John Foster Dulles requesting a meeting in Washington about the trip. Dulles briefed Graham much like a diplomat before a summit meeting. The crusade could not only be an important religious occasion, Dulles told Graham, but also a blow for democracy against communism. The revival would represent not only God but also country.

At several stops on the Indian tour, the tall blond evangelist was engulfed by massive crowds, worshipful but intimidating. Word of his presence traveled like electricity through the villages and everywhere he stopped great crowds pressed in to catch a glimpse of the visitor and to hear his message. Never, said Graham, had he experienced such a sense of the power of the gospel. At times, however, it was as if the crowds were worshipping Graham himself as a deity and not the Christ he was proclaiming. That realization, said Graham, filled him with terror.

While Graham was touring Europe and the Far East, Ruth was in Montreat and the nearby hills looking for the perfect spot to build a new home. It would not be built of new brick or lumber, as Billy probably would have preferred, but out of old logs, used doors, bricks from an old schoolhouse, and other rustic parts from other houses long used up. Snuggled on a 200-acre piece of land in the Appalachians, the home would be "Little Piney Cove" to the Grahams.

Ruth bought antiques at secondhand stores and auctions, and the house began to look like a historic site. Billy called it a refuge. Its living room mantle was made from an old diving board. On it, Ruth had the words carved: "Eine feste Burg ist unser Gott" ("A Mighty Fortress Is Our God").

In the early spring of 1957, Graham took time from his rigorous, self-imposed schedule to spend several weeks at the house. In his diary he wrote how wonderful it had been to spend time running and playing with the children, listening to their hopes and tending to their problems. He wrote about the moments he shared with Ruth strolling through the woods and the surrounding countryside. He also wrote about young Franklin Graham and his continuous plea to his father not to go back on the road. Graham said that he had come to the mountaintop during those weeks and would have loved it if the Lord had instructed him to stay there further. The Lord, said Graham, had not.

By 1957 the Graham phenomenon was no longer national; it had reached areas of the world that no American evangelist had ever influenced. However, the ultimate challenge in the United States remained— New York.

IN THE GARDEN

In the late spring of 1957, the evangelist and his team, responding to an invitation from the Protestant Council of New York, representing 1,700 churches, prepared to take on the city that many evangelists had considered something of a Sodom or Gomorrah. The Graham team amassed a huge budget of $600,000. For two-and-a-half months before the opening of the revival, Graham team members met with church leaders, telling them about the crusade and soliciting their support. In the weeks before the revival began, prayer teams around the world prayed for its success and ministers in the New York metropolitan area encouraged their parishioners not only to attend the rallies but also to volunteer. Bolstered by thousands of people who responded to those calls, the Graham team flooded the city with flyers, bumper stickers, and crusade songbooks announcing the upcoming crusade. Billboards throughout the city announced the coming events.

By the time the crusade opened, few in Protestant circles were unaware of the event. Indeed, it is likely that most New Yorkers, regardless of their station in life and their religious inclinations, had heard that a huge revival was about to begin in Madison Square Garden. The city's newspapers filled columns with stories about Graham, his team members, and the success he had achieved both in the United States and abroad. In the New York *Herald Tribune*, Graham was even given space to write his own front-page piece.

Graham was extraordinarily apprehensive. He worried that he was not prepared for the challenge and that the big city's newspaper wags and commentators might distort the public's mind about his intentions. He knew many would ridicule the revival as a farce and deride the evangelist as simplistic. He told of feeling more inadequate and defenseless than at any time since he began his ministry.

On May 15, 18,000 people crowded into the Garden while several hundred others listened over a loudspeaker in a basement room. The crowd was the largest first-night attendance for a revival the city had ever seen. The crowd was swelled by delegations from 112 churches, mostly from the New York area, but some from as far away as Chicago. A choir of 1,500 assembled.

This was a mature speaker the New York audience heard that night in the Garden, his words and delivery honed by several years of preaching before huge audiences, his manner friendly but earnest, his message urgent. "All your life you've been searching for peace, joy, happiness, forgiveness," he said. "I want to tell you before you leave Madison Square Garden this night of May fifteen you can find everything that you've been searching for in Christ."[1]

When Graham issued the call to come forward to accept the Lord, hundreds streamed forward down the aisles to stand before the flag draped platform decorated with flowers. On bunting behind the dais was a giant placard that read, "I am the way, the truth and the life. John 14:6."

When the service concluded, the team of counselors led the converts down a ramp to a room that smelled faintly of animals. It had recently been used to house a circus menagerie that had appeared at the Garden. No one seemed to mind.

At the beginning of the New York revival, Graham asked his advisors whether it would be possible for a few of the crusade events to be broadcast coast-to-coast. The American Broadcasting Company leaped at the opportunity. At ABC's invitation, and with financial guarantees from oil company magnate J. Howard Pew, Graham began airing his Saturday-night services live from the Garden. On June 1, 1957, and each following Saturday for 17 weeks, Americans across the country could see first-hand what the Billy Graham phenomenon was all about. This was no pre-packaged studio discussion; this was live action from a sporting arena.

The first television broadcast drew approximately 6.4 million viewers. Throughout the three months of telecasts, the viewers sent more than 1.5 million letters and, along with the messages, more than $2.5 million, money that Graham's association used for future work. Graham later said, "St. Paul didn't have television. We can reach more people by TV probably than the population of the world was then."[2]

By mid-June, the crusade had drawn more than 500,000 people, and the team decided to continue until Labor Day weekend. On July 20, the revival moved to another famous sports venue—Yankee Stadium.

It would reach a sweltering 105 degrees in the shade that day in New York, but as early as 10:00 A.M., nine hours before the service, buses began arriving at the stadium. An aerial view of the famed home of the Bronx Bombers on that evening gave every appearance that the place had been overrun. Every seat, every standing room area, and nearly every spot on the field where Babe Ruth and other Yankee greats had performed now swarmed with people straining to get a glimpse of and hear a word from Billy Graham. The multitude covered all of the playing field except for the infield. People even surrounded the famous mini-monuments to Ruth, Lou Gehrig, and others in the deepest part of center field. Stadium historians would later say that the crowd eclipsed the attendance record of 88,150 set by the 1935 heavyweight championship bout between Joe Louis and Max Baer.

After an energetic sermon, Billy introduced to the crowd Vice President Richard M. Nixon, a man, the evangelist said, of vision, integrity, and courage. Nixon brought greetings from President Eisenhower, who, he said, was a good friend of Graham.

So efficient was the preparation for the Yankee Stadium appearance that the collection, undertaken by 1,200 ushers, took only 3 minutes and

45 seconds. That was less time than some small churches took on a typical Sunday morning service.

Through the summer, Graham appeared on radio and television programs to answer questions about the revival, fended off barbs and insults from detractors, and worked feverishly to keep the momentum he had gathered. On September 2, he closed the New York crusade with a mass rally in the heart of the city's entertainment district. The streets of Times Square filled as if it were New Year's Eve.

The 38-year-old evangelist, 30 pounds lighter than when he began the New York revival in May, stood at the rostrum amid the red, white, and blue colors of bunting and flags, the thousands of people waving their Bibles aloft, and the elaborate sound system of mobile loudspeakers ready to amplify his voice through the canyons of New York's skyscrapers. Broadway neon of theater marquees, advertising billboards, and restaurant signs mixed with the setting sun as Billy began to speak. Times Square, he said, was a place of merrymaking, of moneymaking, and of amusement. "Tonight," he declared, "for a few moments it is being turned into a great cathedral as a symbol of spiritual revival that is now in progress in America. Let us tell the whole world tonight that we Americans believe in God."[3]

Graham's association claimed that 2 million people had attended the New York crusade's services and 55,000 decisions for Christ had been registered. A Gallup poll taken that summer revealed that 85 percent of Americans could correctly identify Billy Graham and three-quarters of that number regarded him positively.

The New York revival was a triumph beyond anything that Billy Graham and his associates had ever dreamed possible. With a carefully executed plan, the team enlisted thousands of supporters to carry out numerous tasks to make as great an impact as possible. Graham enjoyed the unprecedented help of national magazines and newspapers paving the way for him to take on this crucial and highly visible campaign. All of the combined effort had worked magic.

THE FALLEN FUNDAMENTALIST

Apart from the staggering number of visitors who flocked to Madison Square Garden and other local venues to see the celebrated evangelist, the New York campaign marked another watershed in Graham's ministry. It drove a wedge between Graham and a base of fundamentalist supporters that had followed him from the earliest days of his ministry.

Graham's breathless ascent to the top of the evangelical world had increasingly left many of his oldest supporters gasping for theological air as the evangelist gathered to his side supporters from various parts of American society totally repugnant to right-wing fundamentalist Christians and their leaders. He had made friends and partners in his various revivals with individuals and organizations—from Catholics to "liberal" theologians—who had varying beliefs and opinions regarding the literal meaning of the Bible and other theological questions.

Fundamentalists occupied a defined world of certainties. Charles Templeton, one of Billy Graham's friends from the days of Youth for Christ, made a list of basic fundamentalist beliefs, as he understood them, in the middle of the twentieth century. The Bible was the rock, God's word without error. It taught that in approximately 4000 B.C. God created the world in five days. On the sixth day, he created Adam and Eve and placed them in a paradise called the Garden of Eden. Adam and Eve sinned, commonly believed to mean that they had sex. Because of Adam and Eve's transgression, all of mankind was sinful. At one point, God destroyed the world to rebuild it, saving only Noah and his family and two of each species. God delivered the Ten Commandments to Moses. Jesus of Nazareth, of virgin birth, was the Almighty God. Having been executed by the Romans and buried, he rose from the grave and ascended to heaven. He will in the future return to Earth to rule for 1,000 years. The wicked—those who have not been "born again," including Roman Catholics, most members of conventional churches, and all the millions who follow other religions or no religion at all—will be banished to a place of endless anguish. Born-again Christians will live an eternal life of bliss, ruling with Christ on Earth for the 1,000 years and then forever in a heaven where the streets are paved with gold. Templeton also pointed out that fundamentalists accepted all biblical miracles as fact, including the assertion that Gideon made the sun stand still.

To strict fundamentalists, these were undeniable truths, the basis for Christian belief. These were truths about which there could be no debate. They were truths that preachers of gospel must advance without equivocation or doubt. They believed that the kind of association Graham was having with liberals was unacceptable. It was nothing less than a sin to give legitimacy to those who subscribed to a less than pure doctrine. No diversion from the truth must be tolerated.

Several things about Billy Graham alarmed the fundamentalists. He had publicly endorsed the Revised Standard Version of the Bible in his Pittsburgh campaign before it had ever been released for examination. This translation had been produced by liberal scholars under the auspices of the National Council of Churches. Similar trends began to emerge in some of the Graham campaigns in Great Britain. Liberal churchmen participated in the crusades themselves. Graham advised converts who belonged to the Church of England not to change their ideas regarding theology but to return to their own congregations.

Among Graham's friends were Bishop Fulton Sheen, whose weekly 30-minute television show *Life Is Worth Living* drew 10 million viewers from 1952 to 1957, and Richard Cushing, Archbishop of Boston and, for nearly 12 years, a Cardinal. Nothing horrified fundamentalists more than Graham's flirtations with Catholics, his cuddling close to Rome. Graham did not disparage Catholics from the platform; indeed, he welcomed them to his meetings, encouraged them to return to their Catholic churches energized to carry out the Lord's work. To fundamentalists, this was playing with the devil. To them, Catholicism was no more of an expression of Christianity than was atheism. They saw Graham's gestures as offensive.

Finally, there was the New York crusade itself. It was sponsored by the liberal Protestant Church Council of New York City, another group of ministers for whom fundamentalists had no use. The council, they contended, included many churches and clergy who were theologically liberal and who denied some of the most important elements of the biblical message.

The Graham crusade committee in New York included over 100 so-called Modernists, many of whom denied the complete infallibility of Scripture. The wife of Modernist Norman Vincent Peale headed up the women's prayer groups for the crusade. Modernists like civil rights leader Dr. Martin Luther King Jr. sat on the platform at one of the meetings and led in prayer.

The participation of outright liberals in a great campaign such as this was a first in American evangelism. Not only were they prominent on the platform—their churches received hundreds of decision cards from the Graham team. Marble Collegiate Church, whose pastor, Norman Vincent Peale, an enormously popular writer and public figure, received the most decision cards of any New York Church. In his books and magazine, *Guidepost*, Peale promoted a philosophy that melded modern psychology and the Bible. This was hardly the kind of Christianity that fundamentalist leaders wished to see in ascendancy.

Bob Jones, president of Bob Jones University, the preeminent fundamentalist academic institution in the country, openly accused Graham of peddling a discount type of religion. John R. Rice, a Texas Baptist evangelist who authored scores of books and founded *Sword of the Lord*, the largest independent religious weekly, a magazine read by thousands of preachers that had an enormous impact on the fundamentalist movement, was an early Graham supporter. As it became obvious that Graham was pursuing an ecumenical course, Rice met with him at Billy's Montreat home, urging the evangelist to maintain a more strict line. When Graham continued on the same course, Rice publicly disassociated himself and his magazine from Graham in 1957.

Radio evangelist Jack Wyrtzen also broke with Graham at the time of the 1957 crusade. "I never questioned Billy's motives," he said, "but I think sometimes it's the end that justifies the means with him." Wyrtzen was particularly annoyed when Graham invited a Seventh Day Adventist to the platform and especially annoyed at the participation of Norman Vincent Peale.[4]

When other hard-line fundamentalists attacked Graham for his New York venture, the evangelist retorted that the sign of Christian discipleship is not merely established orthodoxy but love. Christianity, he said, must not be limited to any one church or any one narrow theological approach. Graham had made it clear that he was not coming to New York to clean it up theologically; he was there to get people to dedicate themselves to God and to go to their own churches, even if they were Catholic.

Time and again Graham acknowledged that his purpose was never to take people out of their churches, but to strengthen local churches, and that he would be willing to work with all that were willing to work with him. The result was that the crusade platforms would often have representatives of many different denominations and faiths.

It was becoming more obvious with each revival that Graham had left his fundamentalist base for a broader movement, one that would appeal to a much wider—even global—audience. It would be a message of inclusiveness rather than division, one that would encourage men and women from all backgrounds and societies to come together under one banner of Christian love despite their doctrinal differences.

In religious circles it became known as the new evangelicalism. One of its pioneers was Harold Ockenga, whom some called the father of new evangelicalism and who had invited Billy to launch the Boston revival in his church in Boston shortly after the Los Angeles campaign that had rocketed Graham to national attention. Ockenga said that Billy Graham personified the new evangelicalism and had become a spokesman of its convictions and ideals.

In the end, Graham decided he could do without hard-line fundamentalist backing, even though it had been a strong bastion of support for much of his career. Graham wrote during the crusade: "I have thanked God a thousand times in the last few days that He gave me grace, during these months of severe attacks, never to answer back. I do not want to get my mind off Christ. We have been promised that if we keep our minds on

Him the peace that passes understanding will prevail in our hearts. This has certainly been true."[5]

Most of the theological tensions and sectarian bickering surrounding the New York crusade had been behind the scenes. Up front, to New Yorkers and the rest of the country, this had been big-time American evangelism taking on America's big-time city. It had been spectacle, show business, advertising blitzkrieg, media hype, and a giant call for national redemption.

As the Reverend Dr. John Ellis Large of the Episcopal Church of the Heavenly Rest said, "Some ministers have used bad taste in criticizing Graham, and one said the Holy Spirit couldn't exist in the Garden."[6] But what started in the Garden of Eden, Ellis said, could surely work in Madison Square Garden. After all, for New Yorkers, what better place could one find?

NOTES

1. "Text of Billy Graham's Sermon Opening His Crusade in Madison Square Garden," *New York Times*, 16 May 1957.

2. "Billy Graham New York Crusade."

3. George Dugan, "Graham's Farewell Packs Broadway," *New York Times*, 2 September 1957.

4. Jack Wyrtzen, interview, (Collection 446, T6 Transcript), Archives of the Billy Graham Center, Wheaton College, Wheaton, Ill., 5 October 1991.

5. Mitchell, *God in the Garden*, p. 23.

6. "Billy Graham New York Crusade."

Chapter 10

A CAREFUL CRUSADE
FOR EQUALITY

In 1915, at a Billy Sunday revival in Philadelphia, the famous journalist John Reed asked one of the evangelist's workers about plans to go to various cities in the South. "We don't know what to do about the color line," the worker told Reed. "We've been in conference several days seeking spiritual guidance." The dilemma was whether to have a tabernacle with separate seating for blacks and whites or to alternate meetings of the two races. "It's very difficult."[1]

For Billy Graham it was still difficult. It had always been so. When evangelists had preached in the South at the turn of the century, they treated the race question with strict deference to the social practices of the place and time. Dwight Moody, for example, had held a few revivals in southern cities and set aside meetings especially for black worshippers. If buses and water fountains had separate facilities, why not revivals?

In 1898, the Supreme Court's *Plessy v. Ferguson* decision legitimized the practice of railroads providing "separate but equal" accommodations for black and white citizens. The case involved Homer Plessy, a black man who, defying the law, sat in the white section of a railroad car. Initially fined $25, Plessy contested the decision all the way to the Supreme Court. The high court upheld the state's separate but equal doctrine.

Plessy v. Ferguson led to more than just separate railroad cars. Schools, restaurants, courthouses, bathrooms, and even drinking fountains were also segregated. The law influenced most kinds of interaction between blacks and whites. The decision mirrored the race hatred plaguing the country; there were over 1,000 lynchings in the 1890s and a series of race riots after the turn of the century.

When Billy Sunday opened his Atlanta crusade in 1917, the city was the center of black higher education and the home of a number of prominent national spokesmen for black rights, including Professor John Hope of Atlanta Baptist College and William E. B. DuBois, a radical organizer, writer, and one of the founders of the National Association for the Advancement of Colored People. Billy Sunday, however, was not about to challenge the social foundation. Like Moody, he held a blacks-only gathering. Fifteen thousand individuals answered the revival call that November day; reporters conjectured that it was the largest assemblage of blacks under one roof in the history of the South. A white evangelist, it was clear, could draw large numbers of black worshippers.

Nearly four decades later, Billy Graham came face to face with a dilemma that had confounded his predecessors. What stance should a national religious leader take on race, an issue that had torn at the nation's fabric since its earliest years?

In 1948, shortly before Graham's emergence as a national religious leader, race was an issue of fierce debate sparked by two significant developments concerning civil rights. The first was President Harry Truman's decision to integrate the army. Although blacks had served in the armed forces since the American Revolution, they were, as in other aspects of society, segregated, assigned to all-black, mostly noncombat units. Living in separate barracks, they ate in separate dining halls. Spurred by the performance of black troops in World War II, by the urging of civil rights groups, and by a report issued by a presidential Committee on Civil Rights, Truman issued an executive order. It guaranteed equal treatment for all persons in the armed services regardless of race, color, or national origin.

The same year, a young mayor of Minneapolis, Minnesota, Hubert Humphrey, led liberals in a successful fight at the Democratic Party convention to put a strong civil rights plan in the party platform. Feeling angered and betrayed by the direction of the party, a number of southern delegates rebelled. Their leader was Strom Thurmond, governor of South Carolina. They walked out of the convention and quickly formed a separate party whose message was simply to denounce race intermingling. They called themselves "Dixiecrats" and they carried four southern states in the 1948 election.

And so, as Billy Graham's star rose on the national scene and Americans in increasing numbers looked to the evangelist not only for religious guidance but also for moral direction, he faced his own personal decisions. How deep were his own convictions about equality, and how deeply would he involve his evangelistic career in considering them? How much alienation would he risk in a political and social cause that was not only divisive but also dangerous? The race issue would bedevil Billy Graham throughout his career.

Graham later reflected on his years growing up and his views of race. "It was sort of an unspoken assumption that we were in a different class," he said. "Whether it was master/servant, I don't know. It was with some people, I'm sure. I don't think I ever analyzed it when I was a boy."[2]

Reese Brown, a former sergeant in World War I, worked for 15 years as a foreman for the Grahams. Billy admired Reese Brown and played with his children. He saw little reason to accept assumptions about blacks being different and inferior.

Attending Bob Jones University for a time and then the Florida Bible Institute did little to advance Graham's thinking about racial issues—both were open to whites only. Billy did befriend a few black students at Wheaton, a school that had been founded by abolitionists. Nevertheless, the question of race and equality was never at the forefront of Billy's life, either during his early schooling or in the early years of his religious work.

In his early days as a traveling evangelist, Graham, like Billy Sunday and Dwight Moody before him, made no effort to change the existing customs of the towns and cities in which he appeared. Although in Los Angeles and New England there were no restrictions on seating, the tabernacle in Columbia, South Carolina, had a designated "colored" section. When he returned to New England after the South Carolina meeting, the evangelist, for the first time, was directly challenged by reporters about the incongruity of segregated seating and the Christian message that all individuals were equal in the sight of the Lord. Graham had no answer.

The issue did not go away. In a number of southern cities in 1951 he continued to abide by local customs. When pressed on the issue again in California, he awkwardly fell back on the defense that communist sympathizers were behind most of the civil rights reform efforts and that only through an acceptance of Christian faith could true reform be achieved.

Nevertheless, by 1952, Graham gradually began to inch away from accepting segregated congregations. Increasingly national in scope, the civil rights fight had become a battle from which it was more and more difficult to hide. Preaching a gospel, the very heart of which rested on the equality of all individuals in the eyes of God, became to Graham increasingly awkward to reconcile with rigid separation of the races. He began to speak out, ever so haltingly, against racial prejudice and against segregation in the churches. "There is no scriptural basis for segregation," he declared at a crusade in Jackson, Mississippi. He told his audience: "It may be there are places where such is desirable to both races, but certainly not in the church...the ground at the foot of the Cross is level."[3]

When Graham's words were greeted with enthusiasm by blacks and when reporters later questioned the evangelist further about his views on race, he retreated, once again, hedging whatever direction he intended to take. "We follow the existing social customs in whatever part of the country in which we minister," he said. "I came to Jackson to preach only the Bible and not to enter into local issues."[4]

These were not merely local issues, as Graham knew perfectly well. He also knew that they were issues rooted in the gospel and that, as his revival empire marched forward, he would have to take a stand publicly.

In March 1953, at a crusade in Chattanooga, Tennessee, Billy finally staked out a position. He stunned the sponsoring committee of the Chattanooga crusade by railing against the practice of segregated seating. At one crusade meeting, Graham personally and dramatically removed the rope marking out the "colored" section. The head usher, offended by Graham's action, resigned. This was further down the civil rights road than Dwight Moody, Billy Sunday, or any other nationally celebrated evangelist had ever marched.

In 1954, the doctrine of separate but equal enunciated in the *Plessy v. Ferguson* case at the turn of the century was finally struck down by the United States Supreme Court. Black community leaders in Topeka, Kansas, aided by the local chapter of the NAACP, brought a suit against the Board of Education of Topeka Schools, arguing that their children were being denied equal education.

On May 17, 1954, the Court, in a unanimous decision, stated that the separate but equal clause was unconstitutional because it violated the children's Fourteenth amendment rights by separating them solely on the classification of the color of their skin. In delivering the Court's opinion, Chief Justice Earl Warren declared, "segregated schools are not equal and cannot be made equal, and hence they are deprived of the equal protection of the laws."[5] This ruling in favor of integration was one of the most significant strides America ever took in favor of civil liberties.

After the *Brown* decision, Graham, pushing for integration in religious congregations, now had national law on his side. Nevertheless, he knew that ahead lay a wrenching national struggle. Already, his modest civil rights stand had cost him some personal friends and brought him abusive letters and even threats. Nevertheless, the evangelist said, "Jesus Christ belongs neither to the colored nor to the white races. He belongs to all races, and there are no color lines with Christ, as He repeatedly said that God looks upon the heart."[6]

As the civil rights struggle in these years turned on the fundamental issue of equal treatment and the policies of segregation, a black woman named Rosa Parks crossed a line of demarcation and the civil rights movement never looked back. A seamstress for the Montgomery Fair department store, Rosa Parks had also been active in the work of the NAACP. She knew well the Montgomery, Alabama, law requiring blacks to surrender their seats on public conveyances if segregated white sections were full. Blacks had to pay fares at the front door and then enter the bus at the rear door to avoid contact with white passengers. She was also convinced that any challenge to the law should be done with nonviolence, dignity, and determination.

On December 1, 1955, she boarded the Cleveland Avenue bus and took a seat in the fifth row in front of the "colored" section. The driver, she remembered, was the same one who had put her off a bus 12 years earlier for refusing to reboard through the back door. The driver notified the police, who arrested Parks for violating city and state ordinances. Parks was released on $100 bond. Following Rosa Parks's arrest, several political activists in the city quickly gave the word to fellow workers to mimeograph thousands of leaflets calling for a boycott of the city buses on Monday, December 5, the day of the scheduled trial of Rosa Parks. They also notified a young minister and activist from Atlanta, Martin Luther King Jr., pastor of Dexter Baptist Church.

On the morning of December 5, King watched empty buses pass by his home. The boycott was underway. Rosa Parks pleaded not guilty but was convicted and fined 14 dollars. That evening a group of black leaders organized the Montgomery Improvement Association (MIA) and elected King its president.

Rosa Parks's arrest and Martin Luther King's leadership of the Montgomery bus boycott were calls to action, catalysts that would drive the civil rights movement for many years. National attention was now focused on Montgomery, the boycott, and the dynamic King.

In the wake of the events in Montgomery, Billy Graham could see clearly that the nation was headed for confrontation. Worried that the growing storm over civil rights would result in increasing violence and concerned that his own revival ministry would suffer as a consequence, Graham, nevertheless, believed that integration would come eventually, bolstered by the moral values that, he told President Eisenhower, were "plain for all to see." The South, he knew, steeped in tradition and reluctant to change, would react to pressure and protest with fear and resentment. It was an explosive mix, both dangerous and challenging. "If there was ever a time for moderation and decency," he told the president, "it is now."[7]

In March 1956, Eisenhower and Graham exchanged ideas about how to deal with the racial issue. The president talked about "the opportunity open to ministers of promoting both tolerance and progress in our relations problems...ministers know that peacemakers are blessed; they should also know that the most effective peacemaker is one who prevents a quarrel from developing, rather than one who has to pick up the pieces remaining after an unfortunate fight." Throughout the civil rights controversies, President Eisenhower tried mightily to remain as close to the political center on the issue as he possibly could.[8]

Graham wrote to Eisenhower on March 27, 1956, that the "Church must take a place of spiritual leadership" in promoting "racial understanding and progress." He said he would do all in his "power to urge Southern ministers to call upon the people for moderation, charity, compassion and progress toward compliance" with Supreme Court decisions. He called the developing situation "bitter" and complimented Eisenhower for keeping "above the controversies."[9]

Three weeks later, Graham reported to the president that he had met with several religious leaders of both races, had spoken at Protestant conferences and at black universities, and believed that the moderate approach favored by Eisenhower had been well received. "I believe the Lord is helping us, and if the Supreme Court will go slowly and the extremists on both sides will quiet down, we can have a peaceful social readjustment over the next ten-year period."[10]

Attacks on Graham intensified. On the one side were those who blasted the evangelist for meddling in social issues and traditional values that had no place in the revival tabernacle; on the other side were those who chided the evangelist for not staking out a stronger stance against racial injustice according to the dictates of his own religion. In reply, Billy decided to sit for an interview with *Life* magazine, a publication that reached millions of readers. He would lay out his own views of racial harmony and the need to adhere to scriptural commands of equality of all under God.

He said that he believed that most southern ministers favored integration in public buses, railroads, restaurants, and hotels, and that those reforms should proceed. He pointed out that enforcing integration in the public schools would necessarily be a longer effort because of the personal dislocation and the need to restructure the school systems. "We have sown flagrant human injustice," he declared, "and we have reaped a harvest of racial strife."[11]

His words sounded very much like those of another southern preacher, the Reverend Martin Luther King Jr. In the weeks and months following the beginning of the Montgomery bus boycott, King had become an internationally recognized figure, not only for his stand on equal rights but for his insistence on nonviolent protest. Despite several bombings of the homes of black leaders in Montgomery, including that of King himself, the civil rights leader had remained a dignified yet forceful crusader, his eloquent oratory filling halls, churches, and auditoriums throughout the American South, in Washington and New York, and in Europe.

King and his followers had battled intimidation with steely determination and economic power. The boycott had forced compromise. The nonviolent marches and protests had raised the cause of equal rights to communities far outside the American South. They and the movement they represented were on the move and gaining momentum.

When Billy Graham began his summer-long New York crusade in Madison Square Garden on May 15, 1957, he had attracted huge crowds and massive attention. He had not, however, attracted blacks.

In an interview with the *New York Times* shortly before his arrival in the city, Graham had talked about Martin Luther King's role in the civil rights struggle, how King had set a Christian "example of love" in tackling a seemingly intractable problem, how King's tactics of nonviolent protest had not only been effective but had thus far saved the nation from what could have been a nightmare of violence.[12]

Billy Graham's salute to King was a remarkable gesture for this evangelical from North Carolina. It was certain to bring him ridicule and scorn from within conservative religious circles and in certain racially charged communities. Still, Graham persevered; he was genuinely challenged to inspire positive black response. He and his crusade organizers managed to line up the support of a number of black churches in the New York area. In addition, a number of black pastors took active roles in committee work for the crusade. However, in the crusade's first weeks, the crowds were almost entirely white.

Graham took additional steps. He sent a letter to a 36-year-old black pastor and evangelist from Cincinnati named Howard O. Jones. The extraordinary message: would Jones join the Billy Graham team as an associate evangelist? Jones had just returned from an evangelistic mission to Africa and a letter from Billy Graham, Jones later remembered, was the last thing he was expecting when he returned. Jones was intrigued and agreed to meet Billy at one of the meetings at the Garden.

Billy explained that he had promised God that he would never again preach to segregated crowds and that the decision had been reinforced in his own mind by the Supreme Court decision in *Brown v. Board of Education*. When Graham asked Jones how to attract crowds to his services,

Jones told him simply that if blacks were not going to his meetings in the Garden, then take the meetings to them. "Go to Harlem."

Graham followed Jones's advice and scheduled meetings in black sections of New York. The young black minister, who had preached on street corners in Harlem and Brooklyn years ago, agreed to join the Graham crusade. He set up the meetings for Graham, even though a number of Billy's workers warned him about the physical danger of gathering in those sections of New York. Jones thought that fear was ironic, considering the fact that Christian organizations were sending missionaries to the farthest corners of Africa to proselytize the faith.

Thousands of blacks turned out for the meetings in Harlem and in Brooklyn, and many began to travel to Madison Square Garden to participate. When Billy invited the beloved gospel singer Ethel Waters to sing at the crusade and she performed a rendition of "His Eye Is on the Sparrow," Jones remembered, it brought the house down.

"When the news broke that Billy Graham was adding a black man to his team, some white ministers objected very strongly," Jones later remembered. Some even said that it would ruin Graham's ministry and some began to withhold financial support. "It was difficult. I was usually the only black person around. I received piercing stares, and I often sat isolated on Crusade platforms because some people refused to sit next to me. After Billy preached, we associate evangelists would leave the platform to help counsel people. There too I got dirty stares from people. I'd go ahead and talk to people about Christ, but it was difficult for me. There were times during that New York crusade when the stress was so great. I remember one time when I lay awake, weeping in bed. I prayed, 'Lord, I can't take this pressure. It's too much!'"[13]

Nevertheless, Jones stayed by Graham's side. Jones said that Graham, too, had paid a price for supporting racial healing, but that his stance in New York had been a model for future evangelists.

Billy's statements and actions on race were making news nationwide. A Montgomery (Alabama) Advertiser article on June 7 reported that during the crusade the evangelist had made an uncompromising statement on the evils and ungodliness of racial prejudice.

On July 18, Graham's New York crusade delivered another strike toward racial reconciliation. The invocation that night was delivered by the Reverend Martin Luther King Jr. Among his remarks, King declared, "Oh God, we ask Thee to help us to work with renewed vigor for a warless world and for a brotherhood that transcends race or color. We thank Thee this evening for the marvelous things which have been done in this city, and through the dynamic preachings of this great evangelist. And we ask

Thee, O God, to continue blessing him. Give him continued power and authority. And as we look into him tonight, grant that our hearts and spirit will be opened to the divine inflow."[14]

This night in Madison Square Garden was a special moment for both Graham and King. Billy was letting both whites and blacks know that he was willing to be identified with the civil rights movement and its foremost leader; King was saying to the black community that Graham was their ally and not their enemy. These two preachers from the South stood together to say that racism and racial hatred had no place in God's universe and that there could be no such thing as a Christian racist.

A few weeks later, King told Graham that the fellowship they shared on the platform at Madison Square Garden had been one of the high points of his life. He said that the crusade had been an evangelistic tour de force and that God had done marvelous works through Graham. "I am deeply grateful to you for the stand which you have taken in the area of race relations. You have courageously brought the Christian gospel to bear on the question of race in all of its urgent dimensions. I am sure you will continue this emphasis in all of your preaching, for you, above any other preacher in America can open the eyes of many persons on this question." Graham's popularity, influence, powerful message, and the fact that he was a native southerner, King said, offered a tremendous opportunity to make progress in a critical area of the life of the country. "Although we have a long, long way to go in solving the internal problem of race facing our nation, I still have faith in the future. We are gradually emerging from the bleak and desolate midnight of injustice into the bright and glittering daybreak of freedom and justice. This remains true because God is forever at work in his universe."[15]

Soon Graham was working regularly with African American churches where his crusades were held. At a black church in Brooklyn, Graham said publicly that antisegregation legislation might be necessary to bring an end to discrimination. "His preaching of reconciliation and his call to repentance," said Samuel Hines, a nationally known black pastor, "have had a direct impact on the alienation and polarization which have afflicted our land."[16]

Graham held strategy meetings with King and the two began to consider the possibility of joint crusades. But the great union of civil rights leader and evangelist never materialized to the degree that both men in those meetings might have at first thought possible. The dreams of partnership were broken in a sea of tensions and practicalities. Although they shared considerable common ground, it was not enough to bridge practical and tactical divides.

Billy's gradualism never melded into King's direct action protest campaigns. King's powerful commitment to racial politics never suited Billy's
primary mission of saving souls. Concerned that a too strident and con-
frontational stand on specific political goals would compromise his own
influence and the power of his ministry, Billy did not join King in the
great marches for civil rights. Although his heart may have been one with
King's vision of equality and justice, he faced the practical issues of racial
conflict with less immediacy and stridency than King. Nestling too close
to the organized civil rights movement, Billy felt, might jeopardize the
mission of bringing the masses to the Lord. Less than a year after King's
momentous appearance at the New York crusade, the civil rights leader
found it necessary to plead with Graham not to allow an avowed segregationist to appear on the stage of one of Billy's southern campaigns.

Had the two been able to mingle the civil rights campaign of King with
the Christian evangelical movement of Graham, the history of both racial
politics and American religion might have been dramatically different in
the second half of the twentieth century. With the enormous influence
that Graham could have brought to bear on the issue of civil rights, white
resistance and intolerance might have been softened. With King's continued participation in Christian evangelistic crusades, with the scenes of
such influential black and white leaders praying together, with the televised images of blacks sitting with whites at the revivals, a greater degree
of racial reconciliation might have occurred.

Although Graham stayed on the outside of the civil rights movement,
he continued to speak out on issues of racial healing and reconciliation
and continued preaching to integrated audiences. His careful crusade for
equality drew fire from all sides. Conservative evangelical leaders bristled
at many of his assertions of black equality and his drive to integrate religious services. Still others saw his efforts as lacking conviction.

Francis Pickens Miller, a prominent Democratic political figure from
Virginia, met with Billy Graham during the New York crusade. Miller
knew that Graham was scheduled to speak in Miami later that year to a
convention of some 10,000 Southern Presbyterians. Excited by the racial
appeal that Graham was making in New York, Miller encouraged the
evangelist to carry that message to the Miami convention.

Miller attended that conference and listened to Graham's remarks. "He
spoke for an hour and a half without once mentioning race relations in
the South. Two or three times he came right up to it, and each time
quickly turned away and ran as fast as he could in the opposite direction
like a scared rabbit. LeRoy Collins was then governor of Florida. When
his turn came to speak, he laid it on the line like an Old Testament

prophet." One of the delegates told Miller as they rode on a train back to Virginia, "Well, Billy had his chance but LeRoy took it."[17]

Miller saw Billy Graham's timidity in the South as tragic. The most popular Protestant speaker in the English-speaking world, Miller said, could have exerted a far greater effort, could have spoken out more forcefully as a moral leader in what was the greatest moral issue of the time, and could have greatly influenced Christians in the South to be more accepting to their black brothers and sisters. Instead, Miller lamented, Graham traded his chance to be a true Christian prophet for fame and power.

However, Graham continued to press for integration. He advised President Eisenhower to send troops into Little Rock in the summer of 1957 to enforce federal law as nine students integrated Central High School. He spoke in Clinton, Tennessee, after a bomb ripped apart a school. He made numerous statements to his audiences and to the press on behalf of equal rights for blacks. He continued to believe that true social change came not by force or coercion but only when the hearts of individuals are changed through religious conversion.

Although Graham's support of integration was constrained within the bounds of his evangelistic mission, and although he continued to receive criticism for not speaking out more forcefully on the issue, many blacks through the years remember the Graham crusades as a turning point in their own racial experiences.

In January 1961, Billy held a rally in Jacksonville, Florida. Linda Belton, who graduated from high school that year, was one of the city's black residents who heard Graham preach. At the time, Jacksonville was a strictly segregated city. Linda Belton was not allowed to drink from the same water fountains as whites. However, on the second day of the Jacksonville crusade, she sang with a choir group from her own church, Ebenezer Methodist. "I just remember getting on our white blouses and blue skirts and seeing the people come down, and I thought it was pretty cool," said Belton. Jake Godbold, a member of the Jacksonville City Council at the time, said the crusade galvanized the community. "To me, it's a feeling like your favorite player just hit a home run," Godbold said. "We were all together on that night—no racial barriers, no religious barriers."[18]

Within the setting of his evangelistic crusades, Billy Graham had, indeed, removed barriers. In 1973, at his five-day Atlanta crusade in the Georgia Dome, blacks and whites mixed with the 12,000-member choir. Black churches worked with white churches and black pastors with white pastors to plan and carry out the event. At a Saturday night youth rally, 78,000 listeners heard the Grammy Award–winning group Take 6. It was the first time many whites in the crowd had ever heard these black entertainers.

When many blacks reflect on the career of Billy Graham and his impact on race relations, however, the tone is reserved. Cameron Alexander, pastor of the 6,000-member Antioch Baptist Church North, cochaired the Atlanta crusade. Graham persuaded Alexander to participate by making a two-hour visit to his church a year earlier. Alexander said of Graham, "Many of us feel that over the years, when he could have spoken out, he didn't address the corroding social-justice issues affecting daily lives."[19]

For Alexander and many other black Americans, the power of Billy Graham's evangelism need not have been limited to the religious crusades and to personal redemption. On the issues of poverty, education, unemployment, and hunger among black Americans, the evangelist could have taken a stand.

For Graham himself the race issue was ever a haunting dilemma. He remarked on a number of occasions that his efforts to open up religious services and his personal commitment to racial reconciliation had been underestimated by black leaders who judged his career to be one of caution.

When Martin Luther King Jr. was assassinated in Memphis in 1968, Billy Graham was in Australia. He sent flowers to the funeral and called King one of the greatest Americans.

A few weeks following King's assassination, black pastors Ralph Bell and Howard Jones sent Graham a letter suggesting that the evangelist and his organization now had an opportunity to step into this great national racial chasm and provide leadership. They suggested that he first commission a film aimed at racial reconciliation in which Graham could use his magnetic oratorical gifts to try to bring healing to a country wracked by riots following King's death. Instead of responding to the ministers directly, Billy asked an aide to tell Bell and Jones that his efforts to integrate his crusades and his increased use of black musicians and the black clergy were having a more significant effect than anything else he could accomplish. This was a call Billy Graham failed to answer.

NOTES

1. Reed, "Back of Billy Sunday," p. 12.
2. Martin, *Prophet with Honor*, p. 167.
3. Ibid., 170.
4. Gilbreath, "Billy Graham Had a Dream," p. 44.
5. *Brown v. Board of Education*, 347 U.S. 483 (1954).
6. Pollock, *To All the Nations*, p. 99.
7. Diary of President Eisenhower, 21 March 1956 (NLE_EPRES_DDEDIARY 5556(1)-DIARY32156), Dwight D. Eisenhower Library, Abilene, Tex.

8. Eisenhower to Graham, 22 March 1956, in *The Papers of Dwight David Eisenhower*, edited by Louis Galambos and Daun Van Ed, vol. 16 (Baltimore: The Johns Hopkins University Press, 1996), p. 2086.

9. Ibid., p. 2105.

10. Eisenhower to Graham, 22 March 1956, p. 2190.

11. "Billy Graham Makes Plea," p. 139.

12. Stanley Rowland Jr., "As Billy Graham Sees His Role," *New York Times*, 21 April 1957.

13. Gilbreath, "Conversation with Howard O. Jones."

14. Carson et al., *Symbol of the Movement*, pp. 265–66.

15. Ibid.

16. Gilbreath, "Billy Graham Had a Dream," p. 44.

17. F. Miller, *Man from the Valley*, pp. 218–19.

18. Leo Ebersole, "Graham Energized Jacksonville in '61 Many Remember That Rally for Its Inclusion, Spirituality," *Times-Union*, 29 October 2000.

19. Kennedy, "Racial Understanding," p. 62.

Chapter 11

AMIDST THE TUMULT: BILLY IN THE SIXTIES

1960: "THE MOST CRITICAL ELECTION IN AMERICAN HISTORY"

By 1960 Billy Graham was one of the most admired men in the world as gauged by the Gallup Poll. Three years earlier, at the time of Graham's New York crusade, another Gallup Poll showed that 85 percent of Americans could correctly identify the evangelist and that three-quarters of them regarded him positively. Graham's opinions mattered.

In the late summer of 1960, Democrats and Republicans jockeyed for position in the race for president. Republican Vice President Richard M. Nixon, whom Billy admired and with whom he had maintained fairly close relations during the Eisenhower administration, easily garnered the nomination of his party to succeed the highly popular Eisenhower. Nixon chose as his running mate Henry Cabot Lodge of Massachusetts, a former ambassador to the United Nations.

The Democratic Party nominated a young senator from Massachusetts, John F. Kennedy. A naval war hero with a relatively undistinguished record in the Senate, Kennedy was articulate, attractive, and a new face to many Americans. He was a definite threat to Nixon, a respected but unexciting politician who had ridden anticommunism to the top of his party. In a move to ensure greater support from the South, Kennedy selected as his vice presidential nominee Senator Lyndon B. Johnson of Texas, an enormously influential figure in the give and take political warfare of Capitol Hill.

The fascinating wild card in the 1960 contest was an issue that had not been a factor in a presidential election in over 30 years—John Kennedy was a Catholic. No member of the Catholic faith had ever been president of the United States. In 1928, Al Smith, a Catholic Democratic from New York, ran poorly against Republican Herbert Hoover. Since that debacle, no major political party had nominated a Catholic candidate.

Billy Graham was now the most highly visible religious figure in America. All sorts of pressures, both from within himself and from outside forces, drove the evangelist in these hectic days before the 1960 election. On the one hand, Graham was determined that he and his career not be seen in a partisan light. Although he often pointed out that he was a Democrat from North Carolina, it was also clear that he had gravitated toward Republican candidates and Republican issues. Yet, if he decided formally to endorse Nixon, Billy feared that he would alienate large numbers of Kennedy voters. God, Graham knew, was neither a Democrat nor a Republican.

Graham desperately wanted Nixon to win. He was personally fond of the vice president and was especially enthusiastic about the possibility of a Nixon presidency. Nixon had appeared at a number of Graham rallies, including the grand finale of his last New York crusade, and Billy regarded him as a true man of God. Large numbers of Graham's religious associates had formally endorsed Nixon and put extraordinary pressure on Graham to make a formal announcement. On a number of occasions, Graham described Nixon to reporters in very flattering terms, pointing to his experience, intelligence, and seasoning as a world leader. Nevertheless, when asked if he was endorsing the vice president, Graham played coy.

Behind the scenes, however, Graham worked feverishly to drum up support for the Nixon team. Even though he left the country for crusades in the late summer of 1960, he made frequent contact with political figures in the Republican Party, making detailed suggestions on tactics for Nixon to use—where to speak and what issues to address. In Montreux, Switzerland, at a gathering of Protestant leaders, Graham vigorously participated in discussions on the ways and means to defeat Kennedy. When he returned from an appearance in Rio de Janeiro, Brazil, he immediately contacted the Nixon election team to say that many at a conference of religious leaders he had attended lamented that Kennedy seemed to be getting a major share of the media attention.

Graham even wrote President Eisenhower to urge greater efforts by the White House in pushing for a Nixon victory. The evangelist, increasingly brash during the election campaign, suggested that the president could make a substantial contribution by stumping in the Southern states for the vice president.

The 1960 election was the first in which national televised debates brought the candidates into the living rooms of millions of American voters. When Kennedy gained the upper hand in the first of four scheduled debates on September 17, 1960, appearing relaxed and confident, he inched ahead of Nixon in the polls. Despite his preaching obligations, Graham continued to act as something of a political advisor in the early fall. Despite his efforts, Kennedy maintained a razor-thin lead in the polls. The 1960 election, many pollsters predicted, would be one of the closest in American history.

Kennedy constantly struggled to keep a step ahead on the religion issue. To a group of Protestant ministers in Houston, Kennedy faced the religious issue head on. With remarkable calm and assurance, he said that he was a Democratic candidate who happened to be a Catholic. He was not, he said, the Catholic candidate. He declared, "I believe in an America that is officially neither Catholic, Protestant, nor Jewish—where no public official either requests or accepts instructions on public policy from the pope, the National Council of Churches, or any other ecclesiastical source...and where religious liberty is so indivisible that an act against one church is treated as an act against all."[1]

To many fundamentalists, this was, of course, mere hair-splitting, a clever defense against charges that a Kennedy presidency would introduce in America for the first time the influence of the pope on national affairs. They charged that on such issues as public funding for parochial schools and contraception Kennedy would be compromised by his religion, regardless of what he claimed on the stump. Against those charges, Kennedy continued to insist that as president he would act according to his conscience and not according to the dictates of the Catholic Church.

After three more debates, the electorate remained evenly divided, with some polls showing Kennedy with the narrowest of leads. Late in the campaign, conservative publishing magnate Henry Luce, a longtime supporter of Nixon and one of the men who through his magazines, *Time* and *Life*, had promoted Billy Graham, decided to make an unusual request. He asked Graham to write an article for *Life*. It was to be an essay, not in the form of a formal political endorsement, but one that explored the life of Nixon in ways that Graham knew him personally—as a man of God, family, moral rectitude, and public service. The article would appear in *Life* approximately one week before the election.

Graham agreed to do it. Because Luce had not asked Billy to endorse Nixon formally, the evangelist's first reaction to the request was that it would not violate his commitment to stay nonpartisan in the political arena. Nevertheless, an article appearing one week before the election, written by one of the most popular men in the country, heaping praise on one of the candidates could be a devastating blow to his opponent.

As most developments of this magnitude in major political battles, the forthcoming *Life* article became known among activists in both Democratic and Republican circles. So concerned were the Democrats over the article that it is likely that both Kennedy and his wealthy father, the former Ambassador to Great Britain Joseph Kennedy, also a friend of Luce, contacted the publisher to plead for fair play. In any case, shortly before the scheduled appearance of the article, Luce called Graham to say that he had decided to pull the piece from the pre-election issue.

In his autobiography, Graham claims that he was much relieved when he received the phone call from Luce. Graham had begun to feel that the article would, indeed, be seen by most who read it as an outright endorsement of Nixon for president even though Graham had not formally made the endorsement, and that the article would have engendered much bitterness toward the evangelist and his work by those on the opposite political side. Not only was Graham himself nervous about the article; Ruth was especially upset, worried that Graham was plunging too deeply into a partisan political fight that would forever compromise his religious mission.

Shortly before the election, Graham asked President Eisenhower to proclaim a Day of Prayer to encourage all citizens to pray that "God's will be done" before casting their votes for Kennedy or Nixon. In asking the president for the Day of Prayer, Graham characterized the coming vote as "the most critical election in American history." Eisenhower, who had already come out firmly against the injection of the religious issue in the political campaign, turned down Graham's request.[2]

In November John F. Kennedy became the first Catholic president in United States history. The vote was extremely close. Of the almost 69 million votes cast, Kennedy won by a margin of slightly more than 100,000. While Kennedy held a wider margin in the Electoral College, a shift of about 12,000 votes in five or six states would have given Nixon the victory.

If Henry Luce had not pulled the article written by Graham praising Richard Nixon, would the result have been different? How many people who read the article would have changed their minds and voted for Nixon rather than Kennedy? How many people who stayed home from the polls would have decided to vote for Nixon if they had read the article? These are historical questions without answers. Nixon himself later said that the publication of the article might have made the difference. Considering Graham's enormous popularity and the vast numbers of people who read *Life,* it is entirely possible that the evangelist's article could have profoundly changed the political landscape of the United States.

After the election, Graham, putting aside his fevered efforts to elect Nixon, managed to establish a cordial relationship with President John F. Kennedy. Shortly before he was sworn in as president, Kennedy invited Billy to spend several days at the estate of Joseph Kennedy in Palm Beach, Florida, to relax and play golf. As Kennedy knew, a public friendship with a man of Graham's popularity would serve his presidency. For his part, Graham was never one to back away from close associations with U.S. presidents.

At one point during the weekend, Kennedy drove Graham around in his car. Suddenly, the president-elect came to a dead stop and turned to the evangelist to ask whether Graham believed in the Second Coming of Jesus Christ. Graham answered yes. Kennedy remarked that the Catholic Church he attended never mentioned it in their services. Graham assured him that it was in their creeds. For several minutes in John Kennedy's car in Florida, the president-elect and America's foremost evangelist had a discussion about the Bible. They talked about Jesus on the cross, the resurrection, and the implications of the biblical message on world peace. Starting up the car again, Kennedy vowed that he and Graham would talk more about those matters someday.

DISQUIETING SIGNS

In playing an intense role in the 1960 election, Graham had entered the world of politics with a driving ambition that surprised even many of his close friends. Always indefatigable in his ministry, Graham was now pushing himself to even further extremes physically, and the efforts were taking a toll. He vowed to hold shorter crusades and settle into a routine of evangelizing that would not drain his energy.

Although Graham's intention was to slow down, circumstances did not comply. In 1962–63, Graham conducted a tour of South America, an area of the world with an extremely high Catholic population and also an area of communist and anticommunist political division. Although the Graham team expected some hostility from Catholic clergy and anti-American sentiment, it did not expect organized opposition.

Nevertheless, in Columbia, the mayor of Barranquilla denied Graham permission to speak in the city's largest baseball stadium and the team was forced to use the grounds of an American Presbyterian school. In Maracaibo, a group of protesters tore down revival placards and distributed leaflets threatening the public to stay away from the crusade. As the evangelist spoke at a government building, a crowd pounded on doors, fired guns into the air, and carried anti-American signs. In Paraguay, the Catholic establishment organized an anti-Graham parade in the streets of Anuncion a day before the evangelist was to speak.

Even though Graham spoke to large crowds in several South American countries, including Brazil and Argentina, the entire foray into this part of the world had a pronounced edge of fear for the Graham team. At one stop, amidst shouting and confusion, Graham was escorted away from a growing mob through a back door. Seemingly unfazed by the commotion, Graham asked his photographer, Ralph Busby, to continue to take pictures as Busby was busy picking up his equipment to retreat to safer ground.

Back in the United States, Graham held a massive service at Soldier Field in Chicago in the summer of 1962 that attracted over 116,000 people, the largest gathering of a Graham revival yet. The following year, the Graham crusade returned to Los Angeles, the city that had launched the evangelist to international renown. At the final service in the Los Angeles Coliseum, he drew an even larger crowd than the one that had filled Soldier Field in Chicago—over 134,000 people, the largest number of people ever assembled in that stadium.

Returning to Montreat, Graham found relaxation with Ruth and the five children, along with a veritable menagerie of animals that the family had collected, including ponies. Except for the antics of young Franklin, who began to exhibit an independence that seemed to take him to forbidden places (he started puffing on the discarded cigarettes of farm workers when he was three years old), the children were a delightful respite for Graham, especially after the South American trip.

By 1963, Gigi, 17 years old, was spending most of her time in a boarding school, leaving Ruth to care for Franklin, Ned, and the two youngest girls, Anne and Bunny. Later that year, Gigi married the 24-year-old son of a wealthy Swiss Armenian. The young man's name was Stephen Tchividjian, and he proposed to her by letter from Europe. Like her father and mother, Gigi prayed long and hard about all of the important decisions in her life and many of the unimportant ones as well. When Stephen arrived in the United States to visit her, she heard God's answer to whether she should marry. God said yes.

In early 1963, Graham, suffering from the flu, attended the annual Presidential Prayer Breakfast at Washington's Mayflower Hotel. Vice President Johnson, President Kennedy, and Graham all spoke. Johnson introduced Graham as that "great ambassador for the Lord."

Graham began his Prayer Breakfast remarks with a dark story told by the Roman orator Cicero about an attendant in the royal court of the Greek tyrant Dionysius in 400 B.C. The attendant's name was Damocles and he talked incessantly about the wealth of the king, how happy the king must be, and how wonderful it would be to live for just one day in his palace. Dionysius decided to teach Damocles a lesson. The king held a grand banquet and invited Damocles to sit at the place of honor. Just as the evening was beginning, Damocles looked up and discovered that a sword was hanging over his head suspended by a single hair. At any moment, all the riches and all the power enjoyed by the king could matter little to him. In modern usage, "the sword of Damocles" has come to mean the perilous nature of life and the imminent possibility of tragedy. Like that sword, Billy Graham told his distinguished listeners at the Prayer Breakfast, a nuclear threat hung over America. To avoid certain destruction, he said, the world must repent and believe. At the end of his sermon, his voice rose and he cried out, "The greatest contribution any citizen can make to the Nation at this hour is personal faith in Jesus Christ!"[3]

Following the service, President Kennedy invited Graham to walk with him to where the presidential limousine was waiting. The president asked Graham to ride back to the White House where they could chat. Feeling increasingly miserable from the effects of the flu, Billy told the president that he had a fever and did not want to pass the illness on to Kennedy. He declined the invitation. Billy suggested that they wait and talk some other time. Kennedy agreed that later would be fine.

There was never a later. The two never crossed paths again. On November 22, 1963, President Kennedy fell to an assassin's bullets in Dallas, Texas. Many years later, Graham still shuddered at the thought of his last meeting with Kennedy at the Prayer Breakfast: "His hesitation at the car door, and his request, haunt me still. What was on his mind? Should I have gone with him? It was an irrecoverable moment."[4]

SLOGGING INTO VIETNAM

In 1954, communist armies in northern Vietnam under the leadership of Ho Chi Minh attempted to defeat the French military that had governed southern Vietnam for 100 years. Outnumbered and overpowered, despite some assistance by the United States government, the French suffered a catastrophic defeat at Dienbienphu, a military base in northern Vietnam close to the border of Laos. The end of the 56-day siege signaled the end of French colonial power in Indochina. The Geneva Peace Accords, ending the French occupation, stipulated that Vietnam would hold national elections in 1956 to unite the country.

Concerned about the inexorable spread of communism, President Eisenhower and the United States helped create the government of the

Republic of Vietnam, or South Vietnam, under the presidency of Ngo Dinh Diem. The United States was thus beginning to assume the role of overseer of the South that France had previously held. When the new government in the South refused to hold the national elections promised under the Geneva Peace Accords, the Vietnamese communists began a guerilla war against the South.

After several unsuccessful attempts to seize Diem's government, communists in South Vietnam joined those in North Vietnam in raising arms against the government. By December 1960 the Communist Party formed the National Liberation Front (NLF), attracting many noncommunists who also wished to overthrow Diem's government.

Concerned that those communist forces would overtake the South, President Kennedy sent a team to Vietnam to assess conditions. Although the resulting report called for a large-scale assault, the United States balked, fearful of being dragged more deeply into the morass that had destroyed French troops. The United States government sent increased military arms to South Vietnam and introduced Green Beret units to help train the army.

Meanwhile, President Diem was proving to be a ruthless and unpredictable leader. When his brother, Ngo Dinh Nhu, seized Buddhist pagodas in South Vietnam that he believed harbored communists, a number of monks responded by setting themselves on fire. Pictures of these gruesome scenes caused such international outrage that the Kennedy administration immediately withdrew its support of Diem and allowed a coup by his own generals. Both Diem and his brother were overthrown and executed in November 1963, the same month President Kennedy was killed in Dallas.

As President Lyndon Johnson assumed the presidency, the Vietnam conflict loomed as the most intractable problem facing the United States. The veteran legislator and vice president from Texas brought to the presidency formidable energy and drive to solve many of the nation's social ills, from poverty to civil rights. Nevertheless, the specter of Vietnam haunted his presidency from the day he took the oath of office aboard Air Force One shortly after John Kennedy's death.

After only about five days in office, President Johnson invited Billy Graham to the White House. "I went up with one of my friends, Grady Wilson, and spent the night there. I remember that we went down to the pool—they then had a swimming pool at the White House—and we went swimming, and I was somewhat startled because they didn't have any bathing suits and you just went as you were. There was a congressman—I cannot think of his name; he was later appointed a judge—he was there

[Homer Thornberry], the four of us. And Grady Wilson told so many fun stories to the President."[5]

The rough-hewn Johnson, who grew up in relative poverty in the Perdernales River valley of the hill-country of Texas, and the evangelist, whose roots on a dairy farm in North Carolina were also modest, would become personally close. On several occasions during the first year of his presidency, Johnson invited Graham to spend nights in the White House. Both Johnson and Graham later talked about the two praying together, many times in the middle of the night. Despite the external image of toughness and power, Johnson was comfortable with sharing his religious beliefs openly with Graham. As the difficulties in Vietnam mounted, Graham shared advice and concern. Few of Johnson's advisers and friends and members of the press corps realized the extent of the friendship developing between the two men.

"Well he had, as you know, an overwhelming personality," Graham said later. "He always liked to have preachers around him. I think he was attracted to me at least partially because I was well known in Texas; I did a lot of preaching in Texas at that time, and I think he wanted to see what made me click...from time to time we discussed the Bible and we discussed especially the theology. He was so interested in his great-grandfather, and of course his great-grandfather held the same theological views that I hold, and it was very easy to say, 'Now, this is what your great-grandfather would have said, would have done.' "[6]

Like President Kennedy before him, Johnson faced pressure from his military advisers to take more aggressive action against North Vietnam. It was becoming increasingly clear to U.S. defense planners that the South Vietnamese army was not strong enough to prevent a communist victory. The Joint Chiefs of Staff advised Johnson to send U.S. combat troops to South Vietnam.

On August 2, 1964, the U.S. destroyer *Maddox* was apparently fired upon by three North Vietnamese torpedo boats in the Gulf of Tonkin. In retaliation, the *Maddox* fired back and hit all three, sinking one.

The incident gave Johnson the political ammunition he needed to justify an attack on the North Vietnamese. He ordered the bombing of four North Vietnamese torpedo-boat bases and an oil-storage depot, an attack that had been planned three months previously, and then went on television and told the American people that the attacks were underway. Congress quickly approved Johnson's decision to bomb North Vietnam and passed what has become known as the "Gulf of Tonkin Resolution" authorizing the president to take all necessary measures against the North Vietnamese. It was the beginning of an escalation of the war that would have ominous implications not only for the country but also for the presidency of Lyndon Johnson.

Graham defended Johnson's response to these events. "The American public was in back of the American involvement," Graham said, "as was Senator William Fulbright and all these others that later became leading doves."[7]

Since the Johnson administration had begun with the Kennedy assassination in November 1963, the president was soon gearing up for the election of 1964, less than a year away. In the summer the Republicans nominated Barry Goldwater, a conservative senator from Arizona who represented the right wing of a Republican Party that was moving steadily toward a more conservative position, touting a robust military and a smaller federal government. Goldwater easily defeated the more liberal New York governor Nelson Rockefeller for the nomination and prepared to take on Johnson.

For Billy Graham, the election of 1964 presented something of a dilemma. Although Graham generally sided with the Republican Party and with most of its stands on issues, his growing friendship with Lyndon Johnson and his increasing access to the White House itself made it extremely unlikely that he would support Goldwater. Nevertheless, the evangelist was the target of an enormous telegram campaign engineered by the Republican Party designed to pressure him into endorsing Goldwater. The massive effort produced, Graham said later, more than 2 million pieces of correspondence.

Graham resisted the appeals, even though his 15-year-old daughter, Anne, publicly came out in favor of Goldwater. When Billy's daughter made her endorsement, Johnson sent a note to Graham saying that, with two daughters of his own, he knew how recalcitrant daughters could be. Johnson told Graham that when the election was over to bring Anne to the White House for a visit.

With the early polling in the campaign clearly pointing to a Johnson landslide against a candidate seen by many of the voters as representing extreme political positions, especially on the issue of war (the Democrats portrayed Goldwater as a man whose election might lead to a nuclear confrontation with the communists), Graham realized that an endorsement of the Republican candidate would not only be fruitless but would also alienate him from his friend.

When Johnson overwhelmingly defeated Goldwater, taking all but a handful of southern states, Billy Graham again became a guest not only at the White House but also at Johnson's ranch in Texas. The two sometimes stayed up well past midnight discussing Vietnam and the various programs the Johnson administration was pushing through Congress to fight poverty and other social ills.

Graham said that he developed a deep affection for Johnson. "I loved to be around him, because I love Texas, and he's all Texas. And I think you have to be in that Perdernales river valley to understand President Johnson. I understand a little bit of the background of where he came from and where his roots were and what made him tick. And the things people thought of as crude were not crude to me, because I had been there, and I knew that that is the part of Texas he came from."[8]

One of Graham's crusade stops in 1965 was in the newly built Astrodome sports arena in Houston. At a climactic Sunday afternoon service, President Johnson and first lady Lady Bird Johnson joined the 61,000 who gave the evangelist a rousing Texas send-off. It was the first time that a sitting president had attended one of Graham's crusades.

Graham took the occasion to deride Vietnam War protesters, comparing them most unfavorably with many young people who had donned patriotic colors and attended earlier Graham meetings in the Astrodome. As he had done for two decades, he continued to warn against the advance of communist tyranny across the world and insisted that the United States must maintain the strongest military force on the globe to insure the demise of the evil tyrants encroaching ever more menacingly from country to country. Our actions in Vietnam were necessary to stop the evil in its tracks.

In December 1966, Graham went to Vietnam to preach to U.S. troops. As U.S. involvement in the war deepened, increasing numbers of young Americans arrived home in body bags, and the political division over the war grew more hostile. The end now seemed no closer than the beginning. Graham, like many Americans, began to experience increasing doubts and frustration. He agonized and sympathized with the president and believed that the administration was on the right side in the struggle against communism. Yet he saw hatred building in the country and was unsure how long the struggle would continue.

When he arrived in Vietnam, he specifically told reporters that the trip was in no way a political endorsement. He was, he said, only a preacher ministering through prayer and spiritual guidance. There were no other motives, he insisted, no secret marching orders from the president and no policy stratagems. He arrived in bad weather that remained bad throughout the trip—a dreary, gloomy rain that seemed to symbolize the morass in which thousands of individuals had been submerged. From camp to camp, the small Graham team hopped by small plane. On one occasion, the back end of the plane scraped some trees and nearly went down.

Following the trip, Billy visited the White House, along with Cardinal Francis Spellman, Archbishop of New York, who had also made a Christmas trip to the war zone. Although both assured Johnson that the troops had displayed remarkable fortitude and that they were winning the war, neither saw the end in sight. Cardinal Spellman advocated a heightened bombing campaign. Graham emphasized that the country was in the right but that Americans were becoming increasingly restless. Johnson, now the target of venomous hate mail and public antiwar demonstrations, already knew too well how divisive it had all become.

The divisiveness reached Graham. In an appearance in London, the evangelist was heckled. On another occasion, when the Reverend Martin Luther King Jr. publicly declared himself against the war in an April 4, 1967, sermon at Riverside Church in New York City, Graham upbraided King for insulting the thousands of black American troops who were giving patriotic service to their country. When the Republican senator from Michigan, George Romney, complained that he had been nothing less than brainwashed by the administration into supporting the war in Vietnam, Graham declared that he had been in on the same briefings and had not been misled.

On yet another occasion, Graham followed up a discussion on the war by stating that his own son, Franklin Graham, was now nearing draft age, and that Graham hoped his son would be willing to give his life for his country. The comment, so personal and invasive to Franklin's life, was the product of frustration. He saw teenagers beginning to burn draft cards in opposition to the war; he saw scenes of youngsters engaged in all sorts of civil disobedience. At one meeting, Graham compared the peace demonstrators most unfavorably with the groups of athletes who had championed the war cause. If only the left-wing radical youngsters had played sports, Billy thought, maybe their political views would not have been so warped. Despite these open protestations of anger and annoyance against a culture of youth he did not understand, the evangelist decided it was about time he learned.

CONNECTING WITH THE SIXTIES YOUTH

Between 1960 and 1969, the number of Americans between the ages of 14 and 24 increased from 27 million to 40 million. But it was not the numbers that mattered so much; it was the spirit of rebelliousness and nonconformity that rocked a nation divided by the Vietnam War, troubled by racial issues, and concerned about the deterioration of the environment. Author Tom Wolfe described the 1960s as the "decade when manners and morals, styles of living, and attitudes toward the war changed the country."[9]

For many young Americans it was a time of experimenting and protesting, a time of questioning middle-class values. The music echoed the rebellion, from the haunting folk songs of Bob Dylan to the youthful antics and lyrics of the Beatles. Many campus protests erupted over the war. Drug use increased among the young. Venereal disease rose and unplanned pregnancies among teenagers increased.

Paradoxically, religious experience also seemed to be on the rise among the young, although not in traditional established churches. The 1960s were a time of impressive expansion for several organizations that were reminiscent of Youth for Christ, the ministry that had introduced Billy Graham to big-time preaching—the Billy Graham with the pastel suit and pomaded hair, delivering the gospel to bobby-soxers of the 1940s in various cities and countries around the world.

Such groups as Campus Crusade for Christ, an international organization geared toward college- and high-school-age youth that boasted a staff of nearly 2,000, became the 1960s version of Youth for Christ. There were others such as Young Life, an international organization of volunteers working with adolescents that broadened its focus in the 1960s to include the nurturing of multiracial and inner-city youth and the Fellowship of Christian Athletes, the largest interdenominational, school-based Christian sports organization in America, founded in 1954. Graham saw the growth of these organizations as an unmistakable sign of the spiritual ferment among the younger generation that was waiting to be tapped for Christ.

Nevertheless, for Billy Graham as well as for a large part of middle-class America, it was a frightening time, especially for parents who faced rebellion in their families. For those involved in various causes and activist work, it was an exhilarating effort to change those things in American society and culture that they felt had gone terribly askew. In 1965 Graham wrote, "This is the generation that will pass through the fire. It is the generation... 'under the gun.' This is the tormented generation. This is the generation destined to live in the midst of crisis, danger, fear, and death."[10]

Appalled at the immorality and license running rampant, Graham first blamed parents who had allowed the young to drift. When he saw long-haired and bearded students on campus and observed the emerging counterculture, his frustration caused him to admit that he would like to grab young demonstrators, cut their hair, give the males a shave, and preach to them the gospel. In a world succumbing to hedonism and other assorted ills, political action and social programs alone were not the answer, Graham asserted. To combat those sirens luring America's youth onto the rocks of drugs, alcohol, sexual abandon, and social indifference, the only answer was Christ. Graham not only lamented the decaying authority of the family but also the laxity of the government in dealing with crime. Along with other conservatives, he attacked court rulings that curtailed public expressions of religion and said that as prayer in schools declined, disturbances in the schools had risen.

Still, Graham wanted to learn as much as he could about what was happening to the culture at this point in its history. In order to connect with these youngsters, he had to find out as much about their beliefs, hopes, and frustrations as he could. He went to a music store, bought rock albums, and sat with Ruth for one full day in their Montreat home listening to all of them. During a crusade in Winnipeg, Manitoba, he decided to join an antiwar demonstration incognito. Amidst the protesters in front of City Hall, Billy Graham, wearing sunglasses, a baseball hat, and old clothes, merged into the crowd and chatted with a number of the youngsters. At the rally of an antiwar group in New York, he did the same thing, this time wearing a false beard. At a rock festival in Miami featuring the bands Santana and the Grateful Dead, he donned his disguise again but this time was recognized by one of the concertgoers who asked Graham to do him a favor: "Say a prayer to thank God for good friends and good weed." Graham simply replied, "You can also get high on Jesus."[11]

These limited but heartfelt efforts did give Graham a sense of the restlessness and the atmosphere of change that were part of these turbulent times. He believed that he was now seeing beyond the youthful rebellion and the quest for pleasure; these were young people, he thought, searching for something to believe in and a purpose for their lives.

Graham began to tailor his own evangelistic crusades increasingly to subjects concerning young people. At some of the meetings, Graham's team estimated that as much as 70 percent of the audience was made up of individuals less than 25 years of age. Graham's film production company, World Wide Pictures, now concentrated on youth themes with such releases as The Restless Ones (1965), a film about peer pressure in a teenager's life in the 1960s, and For Pete's Sake (1966), about family members just beginning their walk of faith against pitfalls that can destroy them or make them stronger.

All across the country, Graham made his pitch to the youth. At a meeting in New York, Graham held "America's Largest Coffeehouse," where amplified folk-rock roared amidst strobe lights and flashing neon messages of "Love" and "Jesus."

Graham even took his message to the campus of the University of California, Berkeley, where students and other protesters were demonstrating against the Vietnam War almost nightly. He urged a crowd of over 8,000 students "to stop experimenting with sex, marijuana, and LSD: Why not experiment with Christ? He's an experience."[12]

For Billy Graham, the overt efforts toward understanding youth rebellion and encouraging alternate paths were not merely symbolic gestures. He was beginning in his own life to face the same kind of family upheaval that was challenging parents across the country. He was now the father of five children. A second son had arrived in 1958, and Graham was able to be in the delivery room for the birth—an unforgettable experience, he said later. Ruth and Billy named him Ned.

For the Graham family, the dynamic was always the same—weeks at a time without the father and then a few days at a time with him. Ruth once told Billy that he had missed the best part of his life—watching and enjoying the children as they grew. Graham's daughter, Anne, often said they were raised by a single parent, "and giving your father up when he spends more time with a secretary or a news reporter than he does with me—that hurts. . . . We knew he preached and he went and served Jesus, so I was glad to let him go because of that."[13]

Later in his life when Graham looked back, he said that his constant travel away from the family made him poorer both psychologically and emotionally. The children, he admitted, must have carried even greater scars. And as for Ruth, Billy wrote that if she "had not been convinced that God had called her to fulfill that side of our partnership, and had not resorted constantly to God's Word for instruction and to His grace for strength, I don't see how she could have survived."[14]

Graham admitted that he sometimes longed for anonymity and that the role he had taken on had personal deprivations. "There is a loneliness to it," he said. "There are a very few people that I can really open to and share my total heart with who wouldn't go out and tell it. I have people sharing their problems all day long, but I, too, have problems, and I have to keep my own counsel. I can only share them, really, in the privacy of my room with God and with my wife."[15]

Graham was beginning to see in his own family the first signs of youthful discontent. Franklin Graham, who seemed to be constantly causing mischief, was nearing a point in his life where boyhood antics could lead to young adult rebellion. Aggressive and demanding, Franklin delighted in irritating all the family members. A poor student, he loved the outdoors but had little use for the things for which America's most famous evangelist stood—reading the Bible, hard work, discipline, and dependability. Like many preachers' sons, he recoiled at the role into which he had been born and, as the years progressed, was continually exasperating to his parents.

Billy and Ruth decided to send him to Stony Brook School, an independent college preparatory school on Long Island, New York, founded to challenge youngsters to know Jesus Christ as Lord and to help students grow in knowledge and skill to serve the world. At age 13, Franklin was bent on serving only himself. The exile to Stony Brook only whetted his appetite for more independence. He began to smoke and even acquired a taste for beer with some of his friends who on occasion lifted six-packs from a local delicatessen. Before Stony Brook School expelled Franklin, Billy and Ruth pulled him out and brought him back to Montreat to finish his last semester of high school.

Things did not improve. Twice he was disciplined for fighting in school. He routinely became a road menace around Montreat, speeding around on motorbikes and in old cars. Much to the chagrin and disappointment of his parents, he continued to smoke and drink. On one occasion, the youngster fled from an altercation with a policeman only to be apprehended at the Graham home. As Billy Graham sought to tap into the life rhythms of American youth culture, he would have a case study in his own household.

PRESIDENT NIXON

Following his defeat in the election of 1960, Richard Nixon practiced law and wrote books. Nixon and Graham remained friends and met at least three or four times a year for dinner or golf in California, New York, or Key Biscayne, Florida, Nixon's favorite vacation site. The two had first met in the early 1950s at the exclusive Burning Tree Country Club in Bethesda, Maryland. Now, nearly two decades later, as they sprayed drives off the fairways or relaxed in clubhouses, they talked about world events for hours at a time.

Even after Nixon suffered an ignominious loss in his run for governor of California in 1964, he still harbored intense desires to win the presidency. With the 1968 election about a year away and the nation weary of war and divided over civil rights, Nixon, an acute observer of all things political, concluded that perhaps the time was right for his entry back into the arena. Nixon asked Graham for advice on whether to run for president a second time. Graham replied, "Dick, I think you should run.... You are the best prepared man in the United States to be President." Like a biblical prophet, Graham said, "I think it is your destiny to be President."[16]

As the election of 1968 approached, whatever confidence the Johnson administration exuded about the imminent end of the Vietnam War had been dashed. The North Vietnamese forces had launched a withering offensive against the South early in the year. The nightly scenes on television of the devastation of Vietnamese towns and the bloodstained wounded being helicoptered into battlefield hospitals were leaving a dark imprint on the minds of Americans. The war seemed never-ending, with vague objectives and purpose. More than half a million American soldiers were still in Vietnam in 1968, four years since American combat troops had landed. Each week about 200 more Americans and thousands of Vietnamese lost their lives.

When Robert Kennedy, senator from New York, and Minnesota senator Eugene McCarthy, both ardent supporters of ending the Vietnam War, decided to challenge President Johnson for the Democratic presidential nomination, they were bolstered by the help of thousands of students and other young Americans. On the other side, Johnson felt the wrath of conservatives who condemned the administration for not pushing forward for all-out victory, whatever the cost. Unable to meet the requests of his generals for an ever-increasing number of additional forces and skewered on the other side by protesters calling him a murderer, Johnson took an unexpected course. He went on national television to announce a bombing halt in the north and also to announce that he would not seek or accept the nomination of the Democrats for another term as president. He would spend the rest of his term, he said, in a search for peace in Indochina.

Richard Nixon entered the Republican convention as the frontrunner and won the nomination on the first ballot. In his acceptance speech he declared that a nation in turmoil required new leadership.

The Democrats went through a grueling primary campaign. Vice President Hubert Humphrey, a long-time liberal and civil rights advocate, struggled to defend Johnson's policies on the war. Many observers believed that he needed to distance himself from those policies if he hoped to stave off a vigorous campaign by Robert Kennedy.

On June 5, 1968, that campaign came to an abrupt and tragic end. Kennedy was assassinated in Los Angeles after winning the California primary election. In August, Humphrey became the Democratic nominee in a divisive convention in Chicago marked by violent clashes between anti-war protesters and the Chicago police.

Nixon began the campaign with a clear lead in the polls over Humphrey. Billy Graham was very much an active insider in the campaign, just as he had been in Nixon's campaign eight years earlier against John F. Kennedy. In a late-night session of Nixon confidants in Miami who gathered to help the former vice president select a running mate, Graham was there, along with aging Republican political warrior Thomas Dewey and Senators Barry Goldwater and Strom Thurmond. Each of the three had themselves lost presidential elections, Dewey as a Republican candidate in 1948, Thurmond as a third-party candidate in 1948, and Goldwater in 1964. Along with a number of other advisers, they exchanged views until five in the morning before deciding on a relatively unknown governor of Maryland, Spiro Agnew.

President Johnson understood that Humphrey was under great pressure to break with him on the war and Johnson demanded loyalty from his vice president. So paranoid did Johnson become about the imminent betrayal of the Humphrey campaign that he ordered the FBI to tap Humphrey's phones. The president also would not allow his aides to endorse the vice president publicly. Aware of Johnson's mistrust of Humphrey, Nixon decided to capitalize on it. He decided to enlist Billy Graham in a mission.

On September 15, Graham, surrendering dignity to political action, became something of a Nixon errand boy. Nixon told Graham to carry a message to his friend President Johnson that if Nixon won and was able to win the war, Nixon would publicly give Johnson a share of the credit. Graham was to tell Johnson that Nixon considered him one of the most dedicated and hard working presidents in history. Nixon also told Graham to tell Johnson, "I promise never to embarrass him after the election....I will do everything to make you a place in History because you deserve it." Graham obediently complied with Nixon's request.[17]

Toward the end of the campaign, as Humphrey did become more critical of Johnson's handling of the war, Nixon's lead in the polls narrowed. At the same time, President Johnson now learned through other FBI wiretaps that Nixon, worried that Johnson would find a way to end the war in the waning days of the campaign, was secretly sabotaging those talks. Through a third party, Nixon had contacted South Vietnam President Nguyen Van Thieu asking him to hold out on any decisions until a Nixon presidency could bring a more favorable outcome. Now furious with Nixon, President Johnson began doing more to help Humphrey. On the night before the election, the polls had the contest at a dead heat. Nevertheless, on Election Day 1968, Nixon held on to beat Humphrey in an extremely close outcome.

When President Richard Nixon entered office in early 1969, he promised to end the war quickly by employing a policy called "Vietnamization," begun during Johnson's last month, a process that recalled American troops to the United States and substituted South Vietnamese soldiers.

Nixon recognized that for his presidency to succeed he had to end American participation in the war but he had to do it without the country losing face. He would end the war, he decided, on his own terms and in his own time, with the South Vietnamese army sufficiently bolstered to defend itself. As the American troops left, Nixon stepped up air and artillery attacks.

Meanwhile, Billy Graham remained a close confidant of Nixon. John Ehrlichman, one of Nixon's closest advisers, said, "Billy Graham was a very important figure to Richard Nixon, as he has been to Lyndon Johnson, and some other people in government. I'm not so sure that Nixon took Billy Graham to heart. I think it was much more a cerebral thing, than it was a spiritual or a soul thing...I think there's an element in this country who vested great confidence in anybody who was Billy Graham's friend, Billy Graham's ally, who took part in Billy Graham's programs. There's a kind of a very conservative religious center of gravity in this country, that was very much appealed to by that connection."[18]

Although he carefully avoided any public policy recommendation concerning the war, Graham continued to offer behind-the-scenes advice to the president. In a secret letter from Graham, dated April 15, 1969, after Graham met in Bangkok with missionaries from Vietnam, he said that if the peace talks in Paris were to fail, Nixon should step up the war and bomb the dikes of North Vietnam. This was an action, he said, that could destroy the enemy's economy. The preacher, the man of God, was thus proposing an action that by the administration's own estimates would kill upwards of a million people.

Meanwhile, Richard Nixon soon found the Vietnam War every bit as intractable a problem as had his successor. So intimidated was the administration about the presence of demonstrators in the nation's capital that he dispatched American troops, some just returned from Vietnam, to protect it from possible assault. Nixon and his aides would soon draw up lists of domestic enemies to wiretap. The man who won the 1968 election on a pledge to end the war would soon escalate the fighting and bomb areas of the world deemed off-limits by President Johnson. Billy Graham remained by his side.

By the end of the 1960s, Graham was, in the public mind, something of a White House chaplain. With offices in more than a dozen cities throughout the world, the Graham organization could boast of operating expenses exceeding $15 million a year. On 900 stations, radio listeners could hear *The Hour of Decision*. A new magazine Graham founded to appeal to lay readers, *Decision*, reached 3.5 million readers in five languages. His film production company, World Wide Pictures, was staffed by nearly

100 persons and produced films shown in theaters, schools, and churches around the country and all over the world.

By the end of the 1960s, Graham was a fixture in American life. For two decades, he had reached a level of international prominence never before achieved by an American evangelist. An investment banker from Greenwich, Connecticut, summed up for many Graham's appeal. "He's talking about a part of America that doesn't exist any more and probably never did. But it's a part of America that people want to relate to—the old-time-religion-Little-Brown-Church-in-the-Vale sort of thing. And let's face it, it's nice to get away from all of the problems of the cities and the universities for an hour and listen to someone who sees everything in such simple terms. Instead of smoking pot, you go hear Billy Graham."[19]

NOTES

1. Gitell, "Faith in the System."
2. Fox, "National Day of Prayer."
3. Ibid.
4. Graham, *Just As I Am*, p. 473.
5. Graham, "Billy Graham Oral History."
6. Ibid.
7. Ibid.
8. Fiske, "White House Chaplain."
9. King, McRae, and Zola, *United States*, p. 743.
10. Elmore, "Vietnam War."
11. Eskridge, "Evangelical Youth Culture," pp. 55–63.
12. Ibid.
13. *Franklin Graham: Profile*.
14. Graham, *Just As I Am*, p. 831.
15. Fiske, "White House Chaplain."
16. Nixon, *Memoirs*, p. 293.
17. Ambrose, *Triumph of a Politician*, p. 184.
18. John Ehrlichman, *National Security Archive Interview of John Ehrlichman*, George Washington University, http://www.gwu.edu/~nsarchiv/coldwar/interviews/.
19. Fiske, "White House Chaplain."

Chapter 12

MIXING POLITICS
WITH EVANGELISM

NIXON AND GRAHAM AT THE STADIUM

In April 1970 President Nixon announced in a television address that he had decided to resume full-scale bombing of North Vietnamese forces. Two years earlier, the president had run on an election platform of ending the war in Vietnam. Now, with the resumption of the bombing campaign, it was clear that military operations had not gone well for the United States. The end of the war was not in sight.

Across the country, antiwar demonstrations erupted, especially on college campuses. On May 4, 1970, at Kent State University in northeastern Ohio, four students were shot dead by National Guard troops stationed at the university to maintain order. The war in Vietnam had now, suddenly, frighteningly, taken the lives of young U.S. citizens in their own country. Hundreds of colleges reacted angrily to the terrifying news from Ohio. Many campuses closed. At the White House, surrounded by hordes of protesters across Pennsylvania Avenue in Lafayette Park, the nearly secluded president continued to conduct business.

Less than three weeks after the Kent State killings, the University of Tennessee, Knoxville, hosted Billy Graham's East Tennessee crusade. The organizers had no idea that the evangelistic meetings in the University's Neyland Stadium would be anything but a joyous affirmation of religious feeling. They had no idea that President Nixon would decide to attend.

To the president, the University of Tennessee seemed a relatively safe place to break out of his relative isolation in the White House. This, after all, was not a campus known for its political progressivism or notable for its anger at the war in Vietnam. It is true that following the news of Kent State a large contingent of students, along with a number of professors, had boy-cotted classes and that some 1,500 protesters had marched to the campus field house that housed R.O.T.C. offices. It is also true that demonstrators lowered the flag to half-staff in honor of the students dead at Kent State.

Nevertheless, there had been no extensive violence. Nixon felt gener-ally comfortable in the South, where his popularity remained relatively stable and where his wartime policies were supported in greater numbers than in any other part of the country.

For the 51-year-old Billy Graham, lean and youthful-looking with side-burns and over-the-collar hair, the Knoxville crusade was another chance to echo the themes he had pursued in other recent meetings—that the youth of America, hungering for identity and sense of family, could rally around a revolution for Christ.

The first days of the crusade in Knoxville featured music legends Johnny Cash, Carl Perkins, and the Carter Family. Although a few pro-testers mingled outside the stadium handing out antiwar leaflets, those who attended the crusade were treated to what they had come to hear—a rousing evangelical show, capped by the inimitable Billy Graham sermon.

On May 27, it all changed. The announcement of President Nixon's visit a day before the event was a last-minute surprise, even to Graham. The president decided that the crusade would be a perfect way for him to connect to the people at a time of devastating national tension. He would become the first sitting president ever to speak at a Billy Graham crusade. Excited but apprehensive about the president's appearance, Graham said to a reporter, "There will not be anything political—I hope—in this visit."[1]

The announcement that the president would make the University of Tennessee his coming-out event enraged antiwar protesters on campus and they reacted quickly. Aided by several university professors, student protesters decided to carry signs printed "Thou Shalt Not Kill" and "Peace Now." Knowing that the national media would hone in on the event, the planners decided not to heckle or chant, fearing that such a demonstra-tion would alienate many from their cause. After all, the crusade was sup-posed to be a religious event. They decided to join in the throng when Graham called for converts but they would bow their heads and make the two-finger peace sign gesture. It was to be a silent, nonviolent protest.

Susan Hixon, editor of the student newspaper *The Daily Beacon*, wrote an editorial that began: "Billy Graham's one-man circus has had every-thing except an elephant. And now he even has one of those."[2]

The student newspaper announced the planned demonstration and reprinted a telegram sent to President Nixon by organizers that declared, "We are angered by your announced presence on this campus and we are outraged that you would capitalize on a religious function, particularly in the South."[3]

May 18, 1970, was unlike any day ever seen at the University of Tennessee. The contrasts were striking. This was a religious gathering. Yet, on the stage at the 20-yard line were President Nixon and his wife Pat, Billy Graham, Senator Howard Baker, Congressman John Duncan, and Knoxville Mayor Leonard Rogers. Among them, only the evangelist and the First Lady held no elected political office.

In the stands were presidential advisor H. R. Haldeman, presidential friend Bebe Rebozo, presidential secretary Rosemary Woods, Secretary of Commerce Maurice Stans, and the president's chief foreign policy advisor, Henry Kissinger. In the crowd were dozens of protesters, many wearing garments fit for a depiction of Galilee in the time of Christ. Indeed, one of the protesters, with long beard and hair and wearing a white robe and sandals, looked as if he were ready to play the lead part. On the field mixing with the demonstrators were dozens of Knoxville police and members of the Secret Service from Washington protecting the chief executive from the motley group. Their signs reading "Thou Shalt Not Kill" had been confiscated before they entered the stadium.

As Graham began his introduction of the president, demonstrators chanted: "Politics! Politics!" When Nixon rose to speak, a number of demonstrators began chanting antiwar slogans, only to be drowned out by a roar of pro-Nixon boos. When the president began, he said that being in the football stadium reminded him of his four years on the bench at Whittier College. Quickly, the address began to sound as if the president were again running for office. Only a few remarks about "spirituality" invaded his string of political references. "His remarks were not as forthright a witness for Christ as I had wished for," Graham later recalled, "but I rationalized that he was extremely tired from carrying many burdens."[4]

Before the actual religious service began, most of the protesters began to file out, singing the John Lennon song "Give Peace a Chance." Some stayed throughout the service and, adhering to the original plan, stood with bowed heads and flashing peace signs. Photographers milled around the crowd taking pictures of the demonstrators. Police arrested nine and charged them with the crime of disrupting a religious service, a state law that none of those arrested even knew existed.

The following week, police made the rounds of the University of Tennessee campus arresting those students and professors whose faces showed up in the photographs. Eventually, most of the charges were dismissed when judges agreed with the defendants that Nixon's speech was not a religious one.

In reporting the University of Tennessee debacle, much of the national press was kind neither to President Nixon nor to Graham, asserting that the event mixed politics and religion in dangerous ways. Journalist and author Gary Wills, for example, wrote a piece for *Esquire* magazine entitled "How Nixon Used the Media, Billy Graham, and the Good Lord to Rap with Students at Tennessee U."[5]

THE PRESIDENT, THE EVANGELIST, AND THE JEWS

The scene in the Oval Office was not particularly unusual on February 1, 1972. Shortly after a Prayer Breakfast in the White House, President Nixon, his advisor H.R. Haldeman, and evangelist Billy Graham gathered to discuss a number of national issues.

The three began their conversation with Graham complimenting Nixon about the moving remarks that the president had made at the Prayer Breakfast, comments that had some of those in attendance in tears. The conversation moved on to Nixon's strategy for his reelection campaign. The president then commented that he was surprised to have been invited to lunch by the editors of *Time* magazine, a publication Nixon regarded as hostile to him personally and to his policies.

At this point, Nixon turned to a subject that had weighed on his consciousness for many years—his belief that the press throughout his career had been openly critical of him and that the press was run by Jews. After a stream of angry anti-Jewish invective, Billy Graham responded. He did not upbraid or censor the president for his bigoted remarks; he agreed with them. Indeed, Graham responded that the Jewish stranglehold "has got to be broken or the country's going down the drain."

> "You believe that?" Nixon said.
> "Yes, sir," Graham said.
> "Oh, boy," the president replied. "So do I. I can't ever say that but I believe it."

Graham mentioned that he had friends in the media who were Jewish, saying "they swarm around me and are friendly to me." However, he confided to Nixon, "They don't know how I really feel about what they're doing to this country." Graham was not finished. He went on to blame Jews for the increasing dissemination of pornography in the country.[6]

For 30 years, the content of the conversation of the three men in the Oval Office that day in 1972 remained private. Nevertheless, as all presidents had done to one degree or another since Franklin Roosevelt in the 1940s, President Nixon had a tape recording device. As the three men made one derogatory remark after another about the Jewish influence in the United States, the tape recorder hummed along, taking it all in for posterity.

When posterity arrived in February 2002, when the National Archives made the tape-recorded conversations public for the first time, the world was shocked, especially Jewish leaders. Billy Graham, for all of the political machinations in which he was engaged throughout his career, was never tainted by charges of bigotry. Indeed, it was his public ecumenism and toleration that had so angered right-wing fundamentalists.

In spite of Graham's reputation, here was undeniable proof that the country's foremost religious spokesman, in the private company of the president of the United States, had engaged in tawdry, defamatory talk unfit for a barroom. The remarks were impossible to explain away.

Over the years, before the remark and after, Billy Graham had not only made friends with numerous Jewish leaders but had won praise for his work to bring all faiths closer together. When the tape recording was released, writers, reporters, defenders, and critics all scrambled to find any public actions on Graham's part that were anti-Semitic. They found none.

Yet, at a time when Graham, as a presidential counselor, could have forcefully rejected on intellectual, moral, and spiritual grounds the anti-Jewish venom spewed forth that day, he gave credence to it. At a time he could have attempted to divert Nixon from this hate-filled path, he romped along with him.

When the remarks were made public, an aging Billy Graham would apologize:

> I had scores of conversations with Mr. Nixon in which we discussed every conceivable subject. However, I cannot imagine what caused me to make those comments, which I totally repudiate. Whatever the reason, I was wrong for not disagreeing with the President, and I sincerely apologize to anyone I have offended. I don't ever recall having those feelings about any group, especially the Jews, and I certainly do not have them now. My remarks did not reflect my love for the Jewish people. I humbly ask the Jewish community to reflect on my actions on behalf of Jews over the years that contradict my words in the Oval Office that day. As I reflect back, I realize that much of my life has been a pilgrimage—constantly learning, changing, growing and maturing. I have come to see in deeper ways some of the implications of my faith and message, not the least of which is in the area of human rights and racial and ethnic understanding.[7]

On many occasions during his life, Billy Graham alluded to the satanic influences present in everyone, the constant battle between good and evil within the human soul, and the need constantly to fight off the dark side of the human spirit. On February 1, 1972, Graham's dark side ran amuck.

BILLY AND THE JESUS MOVEMENT

It is hard to give an exact time and date when the so-called Jesus People Movement began. In San Francisco and surrounding areas a number of evangelical missions appeared in small storefronts in 1967, established by members of the youth counterculture. For example, a Christian coffeehouse called "The Living Room," run by youngsters but also supported by some Baptist pastors, opened in Palo Alto, California. Young people began to mix the styles of the counterculture—the long hair, the Spartan clothing, the love beads, and the music—with traditional evangelical Christianity.

In Hollywood, California, a Southern Baptist evangelist named Arthur Blessit opened a combination coffeehouse and nightclub for young Christian runaways and addicts on the Sunset Strip called "His Place." The youngsters who spent time at "His Place" were mostly disillusioned with drugs and sexual promiscuity but still attracted to the pacifism and the styles of antiwar protesters and street dropouts. They found a niche together in Christian witness.

Soon, the Jesus People were making Jesus Music, a combination of rock and gospel. In coffeehouses and Jesus rock festivals Jesus Music gradually began to make an impact not only on small groups in California but across the country. Such groups as Love Song, Good News Circle, Maranatha, and Danny Lee and the Children of Truth, with their acoustic guitars and rhythmic vocal harmonies, began a musical genre that would continue for decades.

By 1970 articles about "Jesus freaks" and "street Christians" began to appear in such mainstream national publications such as *Time* and *Look* magazines. They brought to the attention of readers across the country photos, interviews, and searching questions about the longhaired evangelists and the Jesus rock musicians. Christianity had taken an unusual turn.

The phenomenon spread even to popular entertainment. In the spring of 1971 the musical *Godspell* opened in New York. Based on the Gospel According to St. Matthew, *Godspell* told a contemporary story of the last seven days of Christ's life. The disciples were flower children singing "Day

By Day" and "Turn Back, O Man" and, in the 1971 New York version, Christ wore a large "S" on his chest, just like Superman.

If Christ was a superman in *Godspell*, he also became a superstar. New York's Mark Hellinger Theatre in New York premiered *Jesus Christ Superstar*, a musical that chronicled the last seven days in the life of Jesus of Nazareth as seen through the eyes of his disciple, Judas Iscariot. Judas, who had come to see Jesus as a scam artist faking his true nature, betrayed his master, an action that resulted in the martyrdom of Jesus. Realizing that God had tricked him into being the tool of that martyrdom and furious that Jesus was now a "superstar," Judas hanged himself.

Billy Graham followed the Jesus Movement with fascination. He had first witnessed some of its members at the 1971 annual Tournament of Roses Parade in Pasadena, California, on New Year's Day. Graham was the grand marshal. Along the parade route, Graham and Ruth began to notice in the crowds some unusual scenes.

They saw a group of longhaired youngsters holding placards with the message "God is Love" and others passing out religious tracts. They heard others shouting "One Way" and lifting an index finger upward. They saw "street Christians" passing out copies of crude newspapers with articles about Christianity. Graham later remembered, "We were made dramatically aware that a brand-new spiritual awakening was on the way." All along the parade route, Graham shouted back at the throng, yelling out "One Way—the Jesus Way." Billy remarked to Ruth that it seemed that they were at a revival.[8]

Graham saw in these hundreds of young people in Pasadena a spiritual awakening and he was eager to embrace it. If some people saw in the ragged, unshaven youth the dangers of social upheaval, Graham began to see these young people as a Christian subculture, youngsters returning to the religious fold after a sojourn into the desert of drugs and dissipation. Shortly after the parade, he talked to members of the Graham revival team about ways to incorporate the "Jesus Revolution" into the upcoming revival stops in 1971 and 1972.

When Billy arrived in New York to begin a five-day crusade at Shea Stadium, home of baseball's New York Mets, he admitted that his own hair was now over his collar. It was ridiculous, he said, for America's parents to rebuke their children for the length of their hair. He talked about his own grandfather, a Christian man, who had a beard down to his chest, a mustache, and very long hair. Billy's identification with the young street Christians made some of his own constituency increasingly nervous. He later said that over 1,000 letters had come into the BGEA offices rebuking the evangelist for letting his hair grow too long. One of the writers even enclosed a check for a haircut.

In the summer of 1971, Graham sought ways to incorporate popular culture in the crusades, especially in Chicago and Oakland. Graham insisted that "these young people are bringing us back to primitive Christianity studying the real Jesus...which we've been trying to do for years."[9]

At the Greater Chicago crusade in early June 1971, Graham carefully tried to bridge a generation gap among his audience. Guests included a young heroin addict who had been converted, a British folk singer, and a variety of music. Along with the usual crusade hymns, he included the 1960s Simon and Garfunkel classic "Bridge Over Troubled Water," not a usual revival selection, but appropriate, Graham believed, for the message he was attempting to convey. In his sermons, Graham incorporated some phrases common among the youth. At the same time, he reassured his audience that he was not advocating that their children become hippies. "Jesus was no hippie," he said. "He worked hard with his hands. He was certainly not a drop-out." The Jesus People responded to Graham. A youth group leader said, "Tell Billy Graham the Jesus People love him."[10]

In the Oakland-Alameda Coliseum, as in Chicago, the symbols and style of the Jesus Movement were not only common in the crowd but the subject of one of Graham's sermons. In "The Jesus Revolution," Graham envisioned a burgeoning revival movement led by the nation's youth that carried the potential of bringing a badly divided country together. Later in the year, the taped sermon was shown nationwide.

Emotionally and personally, Graham saw in the youth counterculture the face of his own son, Franklin and, later, that of his other son, Ned. Although Franklin had agreed to join a BGEA tour to the Middle East and a fall 1971 trip to work at a missionary hospital in Lebanon, his fondness for scotch seemed undiminished as he enrolled at LeTourneau College in Longview, Texas, to major in aviation mechanics. In May 1972, Billy and Ruth received word from the Texas school that Franklin had been expelled. The action was taken for the offense of keeping a female classmate out all night past curfew. The circumstances were cloudy. Franklin had flown a plane to Atlanta with a fellow student aboard when they were delayed by bad weather. Although both denied any improprieties while on the trip, school administrators said they had no choice but to abide by school policy. Franklin left school and made his way back to North Carolina. Later he said that he had never before experienced such shame. When he arrived home neither Billy nor Ruth Graham asked for details of the expulsion.

In the late 1970s, Franklin's wayward teenage years were mirrored by his younger brother. As Franklin had done, Ned turned to liquor and drugs. He later remarked that his own rebellion was not caused so much by his parents as by a deep-seated call to the ministry that he had repressed. Eventually, Ned would answer that call.

In his memoirs, Billy Graham later wrote of the challenges faced by so-called PKs, or preacher's kids. Because of the long absences from home by many ministers and the expectations and high demands made on the children, not only by their parents but by their parishioners and others in the community, many of those children often found the stresses nearly suffocating. In the case of his own sons, Billy observed later, they faced a double burden: they were PKs with a very well-known father.

As Billy and Ruth searched for ways to deal with their increasingly rebellious teenage sons, their struggle mirrored the difficulties faced by families across America. For America's foremost Protestant preacher, the subject brought to his mind the Biblical story of the Prodigal Son.

In the New Testament's Gospel of Luke is the parable of the rebellious son who rejects his father's teachings, leaves home to a land far away, and turns to a wild life. After losing all his riches and his pride, he returns home in despair, repentant and willing to try to win back the favor of his father. Surprisingly, the father welcomes the wayfaring boy back into his home. "For this son of mine was dead and is alive again; he was lost and is found" (Luke 15:24). For Billy Graham, this was evidence of God's patience and unconditional love. It was a scriptural command to continue to strive, no matter how long the odds, to help those children who had strayed. Whether they were his own sons, or the thousands of Jesus People who had returned to their faith, Graham stood ready to welcome them home.

EXPLO 72

In 1972, evangelist Bill Bright, founder of Campus Crusade for Christ, organized a week long Christian event in the Cotton Bowl in Dallas, Texas, for 85,000 youths. It was known as Explo 72. From across the United States and from 75 other countries, members of the Jesus Movement headed to Dallas as if on a pilgrimage.

The young people shook to the sounds of Jesus rockers, heard testimonies from such luminaries as Dallas Cowboy quarterback Roger Staubach, and attended evangelistic training sessions and Bible studies in 65 locations near Dallas. *Life* magazine proclaimed it "The Great Jesus Rally in Dallas."

Billy Graham, who had become something of a hero to many of the Jesus Movement's own leaders, spoke on six separate occasions during the week. He also tried to convince Bill Bright that an invitation to President

Nixon would be in the interest of the rally. Seemingly oblivious to the havoc Nixon had caused at the University of Tennessee earlier in the year, Graham talked to Bright about Nixon's spirituality and how the visit of a sitting president would have significant positive repercussions for the movement. Bright, fearful of the kind of publicity that had plagued the University of Tennessee, wisely fought off Graham's suggestions. Nixon did not attend Explo 72.

With so many young people gathered for so long in Dallas, with kids living in tents and sleeping on the ground and with many missing several meals during the period, the police feared any number of accidents or protests could mar the occasion. Gratifyingly to Bright, Graham, and all those who coordinated the event, Explo 72 came off without serious incident, even without ruffled feathers. Indeed, one of the security guards at the Cotton Bowl later said he had been shoved 22,000 times during the week but that each time he heard the words "Excuse me."

The crowds in the Cotton Bowl during that week rivaled the storied spirit of Texas football crowds. One side of the stadium would yell, "Praise the Lord"; the other would respond "Amen."

The city of Dallas allowed a portion of the downtown parkway to be used for the final day of the festival. An estimated 250,000 people gathered to hear musical groups such as Love Song and the Children of Truth, as well as widely known popular singers such as Johnny Cash and Kris Kristofferson. Jesus Rocker Andre Crouch later called the day the largest Christian concert of which he had ever been a part. After the singing, testimonies, and some remarks by Billy Graham, the lights were extinguished around the area and the youngsters passed around candles and sang "Pass it On."

Although the movement would fade away in the 1970s, the Jesus generation had made inroads into America's established culture that would survive. Many of the youth who attended Explo 72 and other concert happenings in the early 1970s became involved in other religious activities, some as missionaries, others as ministers, and many as practicing Christians in churches across America. Billy Graham's enthusiastic support of the movement gave it a legitimacy that no other religious figure could have possibly provided. In his stance with the young Christians, he showed tolerance and understanding and gave them a needed boost in turning their visions and hopes into positive and constructive paths.

THE WAR AND WATERGATE QUAGMIRES

In the spring of 1972, the country coped with daily news out of Vietnam as the war dragged along interminably. With President Nixon's reelection bid looming, the Democrats selected as their candidate Senator George McGovern of South Dakota. A decorated fighter pilot in World War II, a scholar with a Ph.D. in history, and an ardent spokesman against continuing the war, McGovern, from the beginning of his presidential quest, trailed Nixon badly in the polls. Although the nation was still mired in war, the public sensed that the country was moving forward, both militarily and economically.

Billy Graham shared this general assessment. As he had done in recent political campaigns, Graham stayed close to the action, sharing strategy assessments and advice with Nixon and his campaign organizers. Graham remained convinced that Nixon was a born leader and a dedicated Christian and that he would be far better suited to lead the country than the untested McGovern.

On the war front, the North Vietnamese launched a new and ambitious offensive in March 1972. As North Vietnamese tanks rolled into the South, thousands of refugees fled in desperation. The South Vietnamese Army, shattering under an increasingly devastating assault, continued to fall back.

In Washington, President Nixon, seeking an answer that would not require an influx of American combat troops, an action that could jeopardize his reelection, decided to increase the bombing campaign. Nearly 1,000 United States planes pounded North Vietnamese troops day and night, and, at least for a time, the North Vietnamese advance stalled.

Back in Washington, the election machinery rolled on. On June 17, 1972, one of the machines crashed. Five men in a sixth floor office of the Democratic National Committee headquarters in the Watergate Hotel in downtown Washington, D.C., just off the Potomac River several blocks from the White House, prowled around in an office building wearing surgical gloves and carrying transmitting devices. They were on a mission—to uncover and lift materials from the offices of the Democratic Party to use in the November election. They were working for the White House's Committee for the Reelection of the President.

Although most of the men had former connections with the Central Intelligence Agency and should have been more skilled in their task, their bumbling efforts to steal documents were uncovered by three plain-clothes officers. When apprehended, the men went quietly to the District of Columbia police department. Little did anyone realize that this seemingly less than momentous event and its aftermath would eventually force a United States president to resign.

At first, the break-in at the Watergate was barely a blip in the news. The election in November vaulted President Nixon back to the White House for a second term. He won by one of the largest margins in history and his victory seemed to vindicate his first four years in office.

Shortly after the election, Nixon continued his efforts to end the war both through diplomacy and bombs. On December 18, B-52 bombers unloaded a massive strike against missile sites, ammunition dumps, communications facilities, and other North Vietnamese targets. This was President Nixon's holiday present to North Vietnam. The president did order a one-day halt to the bombing in order to celebrate Christmas Day. On December 26, the bombers were out again in full force.

The massive bombardment once again stirred those in the antiwar movement. Telegrams, phone calls, and letters flooded the White House. Even though the massive raids laid waste to many buildings in the North, the North Vietnamese, with their elaborate tunnel system for supplies and movement, remained nearly as strong a force as they had been before the bombing began.

On January 20, 1973, President Nixon took the oath of office for a second term. A few days later he announced an agreement to end the Vietnam hostilities. The agreement did not settle the main issues over which the United States had fought so long and over which 58,000 Americans had lost their lives. The agreement did halt the fighting and provided a temporary settlement of South Vietnamese government operations. It allowed for the release of prisoners of war, opened the way for American troops to disengage and leave the country, and took some steps toward reconciliation of the North and South. However, North Vietnamese forces ominously remained in South Vietnam and the fate of the South Vietnamese would remain highly uncertain after the departure of American troops. Nevertheless, on January 27, 1973, the peace agreement went into effect. The United States prepared to leave Vietnam.

By the spring of 1973, the Watergate break-in had, through intensive and resourceful investigative reporting, especially by the *Washington Post*, become a nightmare of drip by drip revelations for the White House. The Senate began investigations. The president denied any knowledge of the plans for the break-in.

In June 1973 White House attorney John Dean, in breathtaking testimony before the Senate, reported that President Nixon had been present for at least 35 conversations regarding the Watergate cover-up. The president, said Dean, knew of bribes to keep the conspirators from talking, had approved the cover-up, and, indeed, had been deeply consumed by the affair and ways to deflect his responsibility in it.

When Nixon refused to turn over some of the White House tape recordings for use by congressional investigators and dismissed a special prosecutor established to investigate the matter, Nixon's future as president became increasingly shaky.

The investigative arm snaked over and under all kinds of shady dealings by members of the Nixon administration. On October 10, 1973, Vice President Spiro Agnew resigned over a bribery scandal going back to his days as Maryland's governor. Members of Nixon's Committee to Reelect the President squirmed before television cameras, recounting various clandestine efforts to smear political opponents, to launder campaign money, to misuse government files, and even, as in the case of the Watergate, to burgle. A number of Nixon's team headed off to jail.

In the face of the charges by John Dean and other revelations from the press, Nixon continued to claim his innocence. When transcripts of newly released tapes proved his culpability, the House Judiciary Committee voted to impeach the president in July 1974. The next month, Nixon resigned his office, the first chief executive ever to do so.

For Billy Graham, the Watergate investigations and Nixon's ultimate resignation were shattering. For many years, Graham had personally vouched not only for Nixon's moral character and his spiritual understanding but had trusted his leadership. When the evangelist finally sat down with a transcript of some of the White House tape recordings, he was deeply saddened, even physically ill. The tapes opened up to the evangelist a side of Nixon that Graham claimed he never saw—the profane and vulgar language, the bigotry, and the personal vendettas he sought to end with total destruction of his enemies. Graham began to think that perhaps he had been in denial in his relationship with Nixon, that the thirst for power in his own heart had blinded him to the characteristics in Nixon that many others saw clearly. At other times, struggling to find answers, he suggested that perhaps Nixon at different times had been victimized by demons. Although the voice on the tapes was clearly that of Nixon, Graham admitted, it was not the person he knew. Later, looking back on his relationship with Nixon, Graham wondered whether he might have exaggerated in his own mind the president's spirituality.

During the Watergate imbroglio Nixon did not seek Graham's counsel, thus protecting the evangelist from any appearance of involvement in the scandals. Their friendship was now something that Graham could only look back upon with deep sadness and regret. He would eventually speak at Richard Nixon's funeral.

Watergate had sapped Graham's eagerness to continue to act as a political advisor. The hubris with which he conducted himself in the political arena had stained his legacy. However, with the scandals now in the past, he was free to do primarily those things for which he had felt the deepest personal calling—to spread the gospel to the world.

LAUSANNE, SWITZERLAND, 1974

In July 1974, while the Watergate impeachment proceedings against President Nixon continued in Washington, a group of 2,400 Protestant Evangelical Christian leaders from 150 countries met in the city of Lausanne, Switzerland. The meeting resulted largely from the efforts of Billy Graham. For Christian evangelists around the world, the charge in the Bible to "Go forth to every part of the world, and proclaim the Good News..." (Mark 16:15–16) was the principal calling of their ministries—to travel the globe to spread the message; to preach the Gospel to those who had never heard its word.

In bringing together so many of the faithful from so many parts of the world, the Lausanne Congress, as it came to be known, showed these evangelicals that their common faith and determination gave them a strong sense of unity. They could work together to devise strategies for bringing the news of the gospel to the whole world. The event introduced evangelistic techniques, considerations of strategies that could be adopted in different areas, and discussions by some of the most knowledgeable and influential evangelist leaders in the world.

When the congress completed its work, 1,900 people signed a 3,000-word document that had been drafted by The Reverend John R. W. Stott, rector of All Souls Church, Langham Place, London, and the leading figure among British evangelists. It was called the Lausanne Covenant. While strongly emphasizing traditional Protestant beliefs, it affirmed the need for evangelists, as part of their religious duty, to reach out not only for the souls of individuals but to take an active social role in helping communities throughout the world.

The congress also created a committee to carry on the work envisioned at the congress. Over the decades, that committee and the various meetings it spawned inspired a whole new generation of evangelists. When the congress was forming the committee, Billy got the best advice, he said later, from Ruth Graham. He recalled: "She said, 'Tell it to go forward on its knees.' She said the greatest need is prayer. And I have found that again and again in our crusades just recently in America that where it is saturated in prayer, we see by far the greatest results...I think we are entering a very decisive phase in human history and what we are going to do in the field of evangelism we need to do now."[11]

Back in Washington, D.C., the political world into which Billy Graham had so carelessly and eagerly ventured had crumbled, submerging his friend Richard Nixon in almost unbearable shame. Thousands of miles away, in the beautiful setting of Lausanne, Graham told the members of

the congress that it was a big mistake "to identify the Gospel with any political program or culture. I confess tonight that this has been one of my
own dangers in my ministry. When I go to preach the Gospel, I go as an
ambassador of the kingdom of God—not America."[12]

For Billy Graham, away from politics in Washington, another wider
world was shining. The success of the Lausanne congress would redound
to his credit not only in 1974 but would become a personal, lasting triumph. In his personal life, the trials of Billy and Ruth with Franklin had
reached a glorious turning point. Franklin successfully returned to school
at nearby Montreat-Anderson College, a Christian liberal arts institution,
and in July 1974 had his own religious conversion experience. The following fall he married and headed off to Colorado with his new bride for
a year of study at Raven's Crest, a Bible college. Within a few years he
would find a calling with which he would be associated for many years, a
relief agency called Samaritan's Purse.

"The fields are white unto harvest," Billy Graham declared in Lausanne. "This is a great hour to evangelize."[13]

NOTES

1. Neely, "The World Was Watching."
2. Adamson, "Actions Remembered."
3. King, "When Worlds Collide," p. 273.
4. Graham, *Just As I Am,* p. 544.
5. Gary Wills, "How Nixon Used the Media, Billy Graham, and the Good
Lord to Rap with Students at Tennessee University," *Esquire,* September 1970,
pp. 119–22.
6. Warren, "Derogatory Comments."
7. Graham, "Statement."
8. Larry Eskridge, "Evangelical Youth Culture," pp. 55–63.
9. Ibid.
10. Armstrong, "Christian History Corner."
11. "Only the Holy Spirit."
12. "A Challenge from Evangelicals," pp. 48–50.
13. "Only the Holy Spirit."

Chapter 13

A WORLD OF SOULS TO SAVE

The Apostle Paul towers in history as the great evangelist of the early Christian church. In bringing the message of Christ to the world of his day—the middle of the first century—Paul was tireless, venturing into lands and among people he had never before encountered. He endured much persecution. Speaking before Greeks, Jews, and Romans, he spread the news of the new Christian religion before kings and emperors and before the masses in Cyprus, Corinth, and Ephesus. He took the message to dangerous places and it finally cost him his life.

Nearly twenty centuries later, another determined evangelist began to seek out parts of the globe relatively untouched or forgotten by Christianity. Billy Graham's reach to all parts of the world and his influence in teaching and touching the lives of thousands of evangelists who followed him would be his greatest legacy.

RUSSIA AND BEYOND

Although Russia had traditionally been a country with a high concentration of Christians, the advent of the communist Soviet Union after the Russian Revolution of 1917 had dramatically changed the country's religious complexion. The Soviet government systematically destroyed Christian institutions and their leaders and drove the church nearly underground. For 70 years, the official state religion in Russia was atheism, and Christianity was illegal.

When Billy Graham first spoke in the Soviet Union at a 1982 ecumenical Peace Conference in Moscow, he was a far distance in miles and in philosophy from the evangelist three decades earlier who began his career excoriating the Russians and all other communist dictators. Graham had come to the conference under the auspices of an agreement negotiated both through and around government officials in the United States. The State Department, especially, opposed Graham's visit, fearing that Soviet leaders would gain a propaganda bonanza.

Nevertheless, Graham and his organization managed to overcome the diplomatic hurdles. He appeared at the conference to speak in favor of nuclear disarmament, a political surprise to many right-wing fundamentalist leaders. Why, they asked, was Billy Graham in the nest of the evil empire, this satanic country that was oppressing Christians? Graham began to receive hate mail attacking him for being a tool of the communists.

When Graham diplomatically downplayed the issue of religious persecution in Russia, he opened himself to attack as a dupe of the communists. From the religious right came charges that Graham was at best naïve or at worst an appeaser, being used by the Soviet government for propaganda purposes. He denied that he was either. In fact, Graham felt that the issue of the proliferation of nuclear weapons was so compelling that he needed to do his part to try to alleviate world tensions. During the conference, Graham delivered a powerful address, admonishing nations for not heeding the dangers of a mad arms race.

He later said that the buildup of nuclear weapons by the two major superpowers had become so serious that he needed to express his concerns in a major public forum. The invitation to Russia was too great an opportunity to turn down, in spite of political risks. In addition, this first visit would open doors for Graham to travel to other countries under communist leadership and would lay the groundwork for additional visits to the Soviet Union itself.

Two years later, Graham was back in Russia, this time leading a religious crusade. At Leningrad's only Baptist church, the Reverend Piotr Konovalchik, looking down at a packed congregation, wiped tears from his eyes as he turned to Graham standing at his side. "We know what difficulties you faced in coming here, Billy Graham," said Reverend Konovalchik. "We rejoice that you are with us tonight."[1]

Despite Soviet laws that prohibited evangelism outside church walls, Graham was able in Leningrad to use loudspeakers for overflow crowds. Inside, 2,000 worshippers filled every seat. Many in the crowd were teenagers. Understanding that the Russian people had for so long been prevented from showing their faith, he did not ask them at the end of the service to come forward to the front of the church. He merely asked for a show of hands.

The Graham party traveled to other areas of Russia. Despite the presence of the Soviet police force, the KGB, Graham moved through sections of the Russian population with apparent ease. He met with Jewish leaders and spoke in Russian Orthodox churches that had rarely allowed Protestant ministers to preach. In Tallinn, the capital of Estonia, an overflow crowd of 3,000 people who had been unable to get a seat in the church had to be dispersed by police. Graham moved on to Novosibirsk, the major city in Siberia, and completed his Russian journey in Moscow.

In 1987, when the Russian Orthodox Church celebrated the millennium of Christianity in Russia, the Soviet Union returned some church buildings that had been taken over by the state and began granting new freedoms to worship. The Billy Graham crusade in Russia had led the way. "In some societies," Graham declared, "you cannot go out and preach the Gospel. What do you do? We must wear the fruit of the Spirit, so that people, when they see how we live, will be drawn to the Spirit within us."[2]

Throughout the 1980s, Graham and his organization continued to expand their operations and their reach abroad. In 1986, Graham put together a massive training conference in Amsterdam for over 8,000 evangelists from over 170 countries. The conference followed a smaller version held three years earlier in Amsterdam. With the conference proceedings translated into 16 primary and 9 secondary languages, the participants shared experiences and vision with other grass-roots preachers.

Many of these preachers had never traveled beyond their own countries, some not even beyond their own provinces. For many, traveling to Amsterdam was the first time they had ever been on an airplane. Graham saw these evangelists as a mighty force that was spreading across the world to deliver the message, each of them ambassadors of the Lord in their own lands.

The Amsterdam meeting inspired other smaller conferences in the years following. Thousands of evangelists fanned out across the world from these conferences with new ideas, emboldened by a common purpose and convinced that they were part of a worldwide movement that was gaining strength with each passing year.

In 1988 Graham took his evangelistic crusade to the People's Republic of China, where Ruth had lived as a child. As in Russia, his purpose was to energize local Christians, to give them contacts in the larger evangelistic community throughout the world, and to try to influence the government to grant extended religious freedom. He lectured at Beijing University and other institutions of higher learning.

In March 1992 and 1994, Graham visited North Korea. Once again, Graham's remarks about a totalitarian regime infuriated right-wing spokesmen in the United States. In acquiring government approval to undertake his crusade in North Korea, he held meetings with dictator Kim II Sung and praised the North Korean leader's efforts to establish contacts with Christians in South Korea and the west. He even went so far as to characterize Kim II Sung, who was nearing his eightieth birthday, as something of a grandfather to his people. In 1988 two new churches, the Protestant Pongsu Church and the Catholic Changchung Cathedral, were opened in Pyongyang. In 1989 a North Korean pastor traveled to Washington and reported at a meeting of the National Council of Churches in Washington, D.C., that his country now had 10,000 Christians and 1,000 Catholics who worshipped in 500 churches.

In 1994, on a frigid January Sunday in Tokyo's domed stadium, Graham drew a crowd of 45,000 Japanese. Although Christianity had first been introduced to Japan in A.D. 724, the Christian Church never took root. Its practitioners through the years had been tortured, burned at the stake, and martyred by other horrible methods. Although freedom of religion did gain ground in Japan after World War II, the Christian church never achieved notable prominence. Graham's visit to the Tokyo Dome was the largest Christian-sponsored gathering in the country's history.

Graham's crusades in the 1990s became technological enterprises, employing the most advanced scientific marvels to reach millions of people. In an effort he called "Mission World," Graham launched an ambitious program to use satellite technology to spread the message across the globe. In 1990, he spoke from Hong Kong to an estimated 100 million people in 60,000 locations in Asia. Similarly, a Graham crusade in Buenos Aires, Argentina, targeted audiences across all of Latin America in the fall of 1991.

In March 1995, Billy Graham, age 76, strode forward to a pulpit in Puerto Rico. As he began to speak, a network of 30 satellites transmitted his voice to receiving dishes in more than 165 countries.

As more and more people around the world heard the message of Billy Graham, the evangelist frequently spoke of the responsibility of his fame. "It's humbling, very humbling," he said. "It keeps me and my wife frightened that we'll say something or do something that would mislead somebody in the wrong direction." However, he also said that he would never quit the work that the Lord meant for him to do. The time to quit, he said, would not be until "God stops him."[3]

GRAHAM AND THE RELIGIOUS RIGHT

In 1979, Jerry Falwell, a Baptist preacher from Virginia, founded a political action organization called the Moral Majority. The organization could just as well have been called "Fundamentalist Christians for a Right Wing Political Agenda." Ironically, Falwell had once argued against preachers engaging in the political process.

The Moral Majority mobilized tens of thousands of churches, registered millions of voters who supported its political objectives, and quickly became a force in pushing an array of moral and social issues. It lobbied for lower taxes, a strong military, a federal ban on abortion, prayer in the public schools, and the teaching of the biblical story of creation, as opposed to the scientific theories of evolution. It attacked homosexuality as sinful. The organization became skilled at the use of direct mail campaigns, telephone hotlines, and television to enlist support and threw its considerable political weight behind the candidacy of Republican Ronald Reagan, who won the presidency in 1980. The Moral Majority became increasingly powerful in the South and seized control of the Southern Baptist Convention, the nation's largest denomination.

It did not seize control of Billy Graham. The Watergate scandal had been a watershed for Graham. Although he still towered as the nation's leading religious figure, Graham began publicly to reject the kind of intimate, internecine political involvement that had marked his service to Richard Nixon's White House. "I am out of politics," he said in an interview in 1981. Graham's public exit from divisive political partisanship did not come quietly. He began to upbraid right-wing fundamentalists who sought to escalate the religious-political rhetoric and to institutionalize religious themes for political ends.[4]

Graham lashed out at Falwell and the Moral Majority for its brazen attempt to act as a national moral authority. He declared that it would be unfortunate if all evangelists became stamped with the Moral Majority label. "I'm for morality," he said. "But morality goes beyond sex to human freedom and social justice. We as clergy know so very little to speak out with such authority on the Panama Canal or superiority of armaments. Evangelists can't be closely identified with any particular party or person. We have to stand in the middle in order to preach to all people, right and left. I haven't been faithful to my own advice in the past. I will be in the future."[5]

It was a remarkable public confession from Graham. He was saying that he had gone too far in the political arena in the past and that he had abused the mantle of authority that the country had entrusted to him. "It was a mistake," he said, "to identify the Kingdom of God with the American way of life."[6]

Although the Moral Majority disbanded in 1979, religious fundamentalists were in no way abandoning the political playing field. Indeed, in

1980, a television preacher named Pat Robertson, who had parlayed a national television ministry into a platform for offering his opinions on a variety of political issues, decided to run for president in the Republican primary elections. Robertson's respectable showing in several states energized his followers, and the preacher began to consider ways to take advantage of the grassroots organization he had built for his political run. His answer was the Christian Coalition.

Within less than four years, the organization became one of the most influential special-interest groups for the Republican Party, concentrating on voter education and lobbying Congress and the White House. Using an increasingly well-developed and well-financed network of supporters, the Christian Coalition elevated the so-called Religious Right to a new level of political influence.

Billy Graham was no more sympathetic to the Christian Coalition than he had been to the Moral Majority. Asked whether the group was making a mistake in becoming so involved with the right wing of the Republican Party, Graham said, "Well, you'll notice I'm not a part of the Christian Coalition. I've tried to stay out of those things. Many of those people are friends of mine, and I think that Christians should vote, whether they're voting Republican or Democrat, but I don't think I have a right to tell them who to vote for."[7]

Graham also remarked: "I have serious reservations about religious groups getting involved in partisan politics or saying, 'God is for us' or 'God's on our side.' Lincoln said, 'I'm not so concerned as to whether God is on my side or not, but I am concerned as to whether I'm on God's side or not.' "[8]

Graham's opposition did not surprise leaders of the religious right. They had long considered Graham a turncoat. As Robertson and others intensified their efforts to link political issues with religious belief, Graham was heading in exactly the opposite direction. "I don't think Jesus or the Apostles took sides in the political arenas of their day," he said.[9]

Over the years, Graham had softened his views on a number of issues. His travels throughout the world and his association with people in many lands and cultures widened his perspective. As hard ideology increasingly dominated public discourse in the United States, as supporters and opponents of a variety of issues saw the world through a narrower lens, Graham became convinced that all the answers were not that simple. In his earlier years, for example, Graham had said that pagans in relatively uncivilized lands were doomed to hell if they were not exposed to Christianity. On this and other issues, he changed his mind.

He began to voice moderate positions on capital punishment and the government's role in eradicating poverty, urging more understanding, help, and empathy for those who faced extraordinary struggles in life. He began to decry the tendency of religious spokesmen to pontificate on the subjects of divorce and on the ways to turn around the lives of wayward adolescents. He urged more compassion and less self-righteousness.[10]

Graham had come to see the value of other cultures. He criticized the excessive materialism of America and its growing consumption. He no longer looked at himself as merely an ambassador of America, he said, but rather as a champion of world ministry. "I've come to understand there are no simplistic answers to the exceedingly complicated problems we face as a country—and as a planet."[11]

Three-quarters of a century since Graham first started on his religious trail, the same groups on different sides of the political spectrum still confronted each other: the Chambers of Commerce against the American Civil Liberties Union; the Sierra Club against developers; fundamentalists against scientists; left-wing zealots against right-wing zealots; good against evil; point-counterpoint; and so on. Compromise seemed increasingly impossible. Nevertheless, in the later years of his career, against the tide, Billy Graham sought common ground.

A FAMILY CRUSADE

As Graham reached the winter of his days, he looked back on his career with one great regret—his long absences from Montreat and the lives of Ruth and the five children. Gigi once remembered that when she was about twelve or thirteen she and her father had a bitter confrontation during which she asked him what kind of father he thought he was, considering he was always away from home. "Tears filled his eyes," she wrote. "It was the first time I had seen tears in Daddy's eyes. Afterward we talked it over, and I have never forgotten that experience. It was the first I began to realize as a young adult just how much he was giving up by being gone."[12]

Through the stresses and pressures that had tested their lives, each of the family members made his or her own contributions to the Christian mission. In 1996, at a ceremony held at the U.S. Capitol in Washington, D.C., Billy and Ruth Graham accepted the Congressional Gold Medal, the highest honor that Congress can bestow. On one side of the Gold Medal were the images of Billy and Ruth. On the other side was a view of The Ruth and Billy Graham Children's Health Center Asheville, North Carolina. The hospital was only the latest of the charitable projects Billy and Ruth had sponsored.

Graham was the first clergyman to receive the Congressional Gold Medal. Billy and Ruth were only the third couple to receive it. At the ceremony, he said, "I am especially grateful that my wife, Ruth, and I are both being given this honor. No one has sacrificed more than Ruth has, or been more dedicated to God's calling for the two of us."[13]

In addition to many public appearances on behalf of the BGEA and her charitable work, Ruth published a number of books and poetry, all of them testifying to her spiritual journey. Her life was the subject of a major biography. As Billy often remarked, she was the anchor of the family and of his own work. As Billy's longtime friend and coworker T.W. Wilson said, "There would have been no Billy Graham as we know him today had it not been for Ruth."[14]

In 1996, Franklin became vice chairman of the BGEA board. At the same time, it was announced that he would be his father's successor when the time came for Billy Graham to leave the ministry. It had been a tortuous journey for Billy Graham's oldest son. When Dr. Bob Pierce, founder of Samaritan's Purse, invited him on a six-week mission to Asia in 1975, Franklin felt his life changing in profound ways. Seeing the poverty, famine, and disease wracking the poor on that Asian trip gave him a new sense of mission. Following the death of Dr. Pierce, Franklin became president of the organization. Under Franklin's stewardship, the organization expanded its relief efforts to more than 100 countries worldwide and opened offices in several countries.

Franklin conducted his first evangelistic event in 1989 and, in subsequent crusades, preached to more than 3 million people in cities from San Salvador to College Station, Texas. In November 2000, Franklin Graham was formally appointed chief executive officer of BGEA.

Anne also became an evangelist. She married young and struggled with depression, but discovered she had an extraordinary gift for preaching. However, as a female evangelist, she often faced skepticism and even outright hostility. At a pastors' conference in 1988, many in attendance stood and, in an extraordinary display of rudeness, turned their backs to her as she preached. "They had a problem with it, and so their problem became my problem," she said.

In spite of this hostility, she persevered. Both her father and Franklin said that she was the most effective preacher in the family. "Everywhere I go, I'm invited; if men have invited me, I'm under the authority of that committee. But I don't accept the fact that as a woman I can't preach to or teach men. My authority is the authority of God's Word." In 1988 she launched AnGel Ministries, an international speaking and teaching ministry. She also wrote books on biblical exposition that won prestigious awards.[15]

Ned Graham once said, "The greatest single inheritance I have is the name Graham." His rebellious youth, much like that of his older brother Franklin, did not lead many to believe that this was another Graham that would end up preaching the gospel. Indeed, Ned's oldest sister, Gigi, once said that the ministry seemed out of question—"I thought Ned would be in jail."[16]

After receiving a communications degree from Pacific Lutheran University in 1985, Ned attended Fuller Theological Seminary's extension program in Seattle and later became a pastor of adult ministries at Grace Community Church in Auburn, Washington. In May 1991, he became president of East Gates International, a religious nonprofit corporation located in Washington State whose primary purpose is to have a positive impact on China's religious history. Under Ned's leadership, East Gates forged a new ministry frontier in China, where a rapidly growing church had an urgent need for more Bibles. Project Light has made possible the printing and distribution of more than 2 million Bibles to Christians in China since 1992.

Although personal difficulties continued to plague Ned, including a divorce in which he admitted to problems with alcohol and drugs, his work with East Gates moved forward. He was joined at East Gates by sisters Ruth and Gigi.

Gigi, who, like her sisters, married in her teenage years, lived for a period in Switzerland and Israel. In addition to raising seven children, she authored seven books and appeared at women's conferences and on national radio and television, discussing women, families, and the issues they confront. Like her sister Anne, she won several writing awards.

Ruth, the youngest of the Graham sisters, overcame a difficult first marriage. When she was 40 years old, she returned to school, graduating from Mary Baldwin College. She married a second time and had four children. She also turned to writing and speaking on issues of modern life and Christian growth.

Throughout his ministry, Billy Graham, as no other preacher before him, inspired and influenced evangelists across the world. Through pressures and unreasonable expectations, through trials and continuing expression of unconditional love, Billy and Ruth also powerfully influenced their children. Their religious mission became a family one.

REMEMBERING

In 2001 Billy Graham returned to Louisville, Kentucky, to preach. Graham's sermon delivery was now more strained than it was during his 1954 visit, his movements halting. He was still a powerful presence, but no longer the 37 year old who prowled cat-like across the platform and punctured the air with slashing arm movements and a rapid pace that left the audience breathless.

Some of the city's residents whose lives were touched by his crusade nearly half a century before reflected on what the experience had meant to them.

Linda Otterback was 12 years old when the Graham revival came to Louisville in 1956. She volunteered to stuff envelopes for the 2001 crusade, to sing in the crusade choir, and counsel new converts. She wanted to do as much as she could, she said, to repay Billy Graham for what he had done for her life.

Kitty Keeley, now 71, still cherished an autographed Bible and a letter from Graham sent to her by the evangelist after the first Louisville crusade. Kitty and her husband Hal met Graham at the revival. "I have a lot of sweet memories from those days," Kitty Keeley said. At the first crusade, Hal had told her not to embarrass him by walking forward at the end of the service. However, when the evangelist made the call for converts, they both marched forward side by side. Hal became an elder in a church, enrolled in Louisville Presbyterian Theological Seminary, and became a pastor as well as a counselor of alcoholics. "His life was changed by the Billy Graham crusade," said Kitty Keeley of her late husband, "and mine too."[17]

Mary E. Curtsinger first heard the hymn "How Great Thou Art" at the Louisville crusade. "I still get a lump in my throat every time I hear 'How Great Thou Art,'" she said. "My dad died in 1959—just three years after singing in the 1956 Billy Graham Crusade Choir."[18]

When Lillian Beckner attended the 1956 rally, she stood in a hallway during the service trying to calm Mark, her baby boy. She remembered that when Graham walked by, she whispered to her son, "Mark, you probably won't remember this, but there goes Billy Graham. He's a great man."[19]

The scene in Louisville had been played out for half a century, from small towns to large cities, from the heart of the United States to the heart of Russia. The massive crowd gathers. Cliff Barrows leads a choir of several thousand; George Beverly Shea sings favorite old hymns in his rich bass-baritone; and celebrities give testimony about their faith. Then the evangelist steps forward. Tall and blond, athletic-looking, one hand in the air grasping a Bible, his voice rising and falling, he wrings emotion from the audience in a stirring affirmation of faith. He calls for converts. Rising from their seats, the people come to him from all parts of the crowd, joining the others at the platform. Young and old, in groups of people and singly, they gather together, slowly walking to the words of the old English hymn "Just As I Am," written by Charlotte Elliott in 1836:

"Oh Lamb of God, I come, I come!"[20]

The people profess their faith in the stadiums; or perhaps they quietly feel a change in their lives in a bar or in their living rooms. Wherever they are, in a tabernacle or in front of a television, they accept the call to the Lord's service from Billy Graham, the Apostle Paul of the twentieth century.

Into the new century, the world's foremost Christian evangelist continues to spread his message of spiritual regeneration and the hope that people around the world may find greater peace and fulfillment.

Billy Graham refuses to stop preaching, even though he is wracked by Parkinson's disease, a debilitating illness that produces visible shaking, and even though he is becoming increasingly deaf. Although Franklin Graham directs most of the organization's work, Billy carries on his calling from the revival platform.

In 2003, Graham filled stadiums night after night in Oklahoma City and San Diego, demonstrating again that his power and that of his evangelistic organization remains undiminished after half a century. Pastor David Jeremiah, reflecting on the astonishing cooperation of San Diego's church and community leaders and the massive outpouring of volunteer help, called that revival "The greatest spiritual event in San Diego history."[21]

As Billy and Ruth live out their days in their rustic Montreat home, the work continues. While planning yet another revival for 2004, the 84-year-old evangelist told reporters, "Spiritually, I feel tremendously exhilarated."[22] Billy Graham, as always, holds fast to his calling.

NOTES

1. Ostling, "Billy Graham's Mission Impossible," p. 48.
2. Ibid.
3. Otto, "Lord's Top Salesman," p. 919.
4. Michaels, "Not God's Only Kingdom," pp. 6–7.
5. Ibid.
6. Ibid.
7. Jordan, "Conversation with Billy Graham."
8. "Billy Graham: Churches Should Shun Partisan Politics," p. 12.

9. Banks and Taylor, "Bigotry a Sin," p. 19.
10. Wacker, "Charles Atlas with a Halo," pp. 336–41.
11. Michaels, "Not God's Only Kingdom," p. 7.
12. Busby, *God's Ambassador*, p. 235.
13. Ibid., p. 260.
14. Martin, *Prophet with Honor*, p. 598.
15. Zorba, "Angel in the Pulpit," p. 57.
16. Both quotes from Bishop, "God's Ambassador to China," p. 22.
17. Smith, "1956 Crusade."
18. Ibid.
19. Ibid.
20. Elliott, "Just as I Am."
21. "Mission San Diego."
22. "At 84."

SELECTED BIBLIOGRAPHY

BOOKS

Ambrose, Stephen E. *Nixon*. Vol. 2, *The Triumph of a Politician, 1962–1972*. New York: Simon & Schuster, 1989.

Armstrong, Ben. *The Electric Church*. Nashville, Tenn.: Thomas Nelson Publishers, 1979.

Blumhofer, Edith L., and Randall Balmer, eds. *Modern Christian Revivals*. Urbana: University of Illinois Press, 1993.

Bruns, Roger A. *Preacher: Billy Sunday and Big-Time American Evangelism*. Urbana: University of Illinois Press, 2002.

Busby, Russ. *Billy Graham, God's Ambassador: A Lifelong Mission of Giving Hope to the World as Witnessed by Photographer Russ Busby*. Minneapolis: Tehabi Books, Billy Graham Evangelistic Association, 1999.

Carson, Clayborne, Susan Carson, Adrienne Clay, Virginia Shadron, and Kieran Taylor, eds. *The Papers of Martin Luther King, Jr.* Vol. 4, *Symbol of the Movement, January 1957–December 1958*. Berkeley: University of California Press, 2000.

Cornwell, Patricia Daniels. *Ruth, a Portrait: The Story of Ruth Bell Graham*. New York: Doubleday, 1997.

Dorsett, Lyle W. *Billy Sunday and the Redemption of Urban America*. Grand Rapids, Mich.: William B. Eerdmans Publishing Co., 1991.

Drummond, Lewis A. *The Evangelist—The Worldwide Impact of Billy Graham*. Nashville, Tenn.: Word Publishing, 2001.

Falwell, Jerry. *Strength for the Journey: An Autobiography*. New York: Simon & Schuster, 1987.

Frady, Marshall. *Billy Graham: A Parable of American Righteousness*. Boston: Little, Brown, 1977.

Frankl, Razelle. *Televangelism*. Carbondale: Southern Illinois University Press, 1987.

Galamabos, Louis, ed. *The Papers of Dwight David Eisenhower*. Vol. 13. Baltimore: Johns Hopkins University Press, 1989.

Gallup, George Jr., and Jim Castelli. *The People's Religion: American Faith in the 90's*. New York: Macmillan, 1989.

Graham, Billy. *Just As I Am: The Autobiography of Billy Graham*. New York: HarperPaperbacks, 1997.

———. *Peace with God*. Nashville, Tenn.: W Publishing Group, 1953.

———. *Revival in Our Time*. New York: Van Kampen Press, 1950.

———. *World Aflame*. Minneapolis, Minn.: The Billy Graham Evangelistic Association, 1965.

Graham, Franklin. *Rebel with a Cause*. Nashville, Tenn.: Thomas Nelson Publishers, 1995.

Graham, Ruth Bell. *Prayers from a Mother's Heart*. Nashville, Tenn.: Thomas Nelson Publishers, 1999.

Gullen, Karen. *Billy Sunday Speaks*. New York: Chelsea House Publishers, 1970.

Hadden, Jeffrey, and Anson Shupe. *Televangelism: Power and Politics on God's Frontier*. New York: Henry Holt and Company, 1988.

High, Stanley. *Billy Graham*. New York: McGraw Hill, 1956.

King, David, Norman McRae, and Jaye Zola. *The United States and Its People*. New York: Addison-Wesley Publishing Company, 1995.

Martin, William C. *A Prophet with Honor: The Billy Graham Story*. New York: William Morrow, 1991.

Marty, Martin. *Pilgrims in Their Own Land: 500 Years of Religion in America*. New York: Penguin Books, 1984.

McLaughlin, William G. *Billy Graham: Revivalist in a Secular Age*. New York: Ronald Press Company, 1960.

Miller, Francis Pickens. *Man from the Valley: Memoirs of a Twentieth Century Virginian*. Chapel Hill: University of North Carolina Press, 1971.

Miller, Merle. *Plain Speaking: An Oral Biography of Harry S. Truman*. New York: Berkeley Publishing, 1985.

Mitchell, Curtis. *God in the Garden: The Story of the Billy Graham New York Crusade*. Garden City, N.Y.: Doubleday, 1957.

Naftali, Timothy, and Philip Zelikow, eds. *The Presidential Recordings: John F. Kennedy, The Great Crises*. Vol. 2. New York: W. W. Norton & Company, 2001.

Nixon, Richard. *The Memoirs of Richard Nixon*. Melbourne: Macmillan, 1978.

Pollock, John. *Billy Graham: The Authorized Biography*. New York: McGraw Hill, 1966.

———. *To All the Nations: The Billy Graham Story*. Cambridge, Mass.: Harper & Row, 1985.

Ribuffo, Leo. *The Old Christian Right: The Protestant Far Right from the Great Depression to the Cold War*. Philadelphia: Temple University Press, 1983.

Scharpff, Paulus. *History of Evangelism*. Grand Rapids, Mich.: William B. Eerdmans Publishing Company, 1966.

Streiker, Lowell D., and Gerald S. Strober. *Religion and the New Majority: Billy Graham, Middle America, and the Politics of the 70s*. New York: Association Press, 1972.

Weisberger, Bernard. *They Gathered at the River: The Story of the Great Revivalists and Their Impact upon Religion in America*. Boston: Little, Brown, 1958.

PERIODICALS

Adamson, June. "Actions of Past Editors Remembered." *The* (Knoxville) *Daily Beacon*, 25 August 1995.

Banks, Adelle M., and LaTonya Taylor. "Graham Calls Bigotry a Sin: Evangelist Calls for Racial Healing." *Christianity Today*, 5 August 2002, p. 19.

Barbee, Darren. "Reverend Billy Graham Has History of Financial Openness, Accountability." *Knight Ridder/Tribune Business News*, 13 October 2002.

Bell, L. Nelson. "A Layman and His Faith." *Christianity Today*, 18 July 1960, p. 19.

"Billy Graham: Churches Should Shun Partisan Politics." *U.S. News & World Report*, 8 October 1984, p. 12.

"Billy Graham Makes Plea for End to Intolerance." *Life*, 1 October 1956, p. 139.

"Billy in Dixie: South Carolina Gives Revivalist Biggest Crowd He Has Ever Pulled." *Life*, 27 March 1950, p. 55.

Bishop, Randy. "Ned Graham: God's Ambassador to China: Billy Graham's youngest Son Is Changing Church History through Prayer and Diplomacy." *Christian Reader*, July/August 1998, p. 22.

"A Challenge from Evangelicals." *Time*, 5 August 1974, pp. 48–50.

Eskridge, Larry. "'One Way,' Billy Graham, the Jesus Generation, and the Idea of an Evangelical Youth Culture." *Church History*, March 1998, pp. 48–50.

Gilbreath, Edward. "Billy Graham Had a Dream." *Christianity Today*, 12 January 1998, p. 44.

Kennedy, John W. "'Deeper than a Handshake': Atlantans, Black and White, Strive for Racial Understanding." *Christianity Today*, 12 December 1994, p. 62.

King, Randall E. "When Worlds Collide: Politics, Media, and Religion: the 1970 East Tennessee Billy Graham Crusade." *Journal of Church & State* 39 (1997): 273.

Michaels, Marguerite. "Billy Graham: America Is Not God's Only Kingdom." *Parade*, 1 February 1981, pp. 6–7.

Neely, Jack. "The World Was Watching: Both Sides of the Picket Lines Recall the Most Explosive Student Protests in IT History." *Knoxville Weekly Wire*, 22 May 2000.

Ostling, Richard M. "Billy Graham's Mission Impossible." *Time*, 24 September 1984, p. 48.

Otto, Mary. "Billy Graham, the Lord's Top Salesman, Says He'll Preach till God Stops Him." *Knight Ridder/Tribune News Service*, 19 September 1996, p. 919.

Reed, John. "Back of Billy Sunday." *Metropolitan Magazine*, May 1915, p. 12.

"Reverend Billy Graham and Ruth Bell: Uplifted by Faith, They Tended Their Union through Hardship and Separation." *People Weekly*, 12 February 1996, p. 155.

Smith, Peter. "Billy Graham: 1956 Crusade Left Legacy of Changed Lives: Evangelist's Return to Louisville Brings a Flood of Memories." *The Courier-Journal*, 17 June 2001.

Wacker, Grant. "Charles Atlas with a Halo: America's Billy Graham." *The Christian Century*, 1 April 1992, pp. 336–41.

Warren, James. "Nixon, Billy Graham Make Derogatory Comments about Jews on Tapes." *Chicago Tribune*, 28 February 2002.

Zorba, Wendy Murray. "Angel in the Pulpit." *Christianity Today*, 5 April 1999, p. 57.

INTERNET SOURCES

Armstrong, Chris. "Christian History Corner: 'Tell Billy Graham the Jesus People Love Him.'" *Christianity Today*, 9 December 2002, http://www.christianitytoday.com/ct/2002/148/52.0.html.

"At 84, the Rev. Billy Graham Still Not Ready to Stop Preaching," http://www.msnbc.com/local/KJRH/At84theThe.asp.

"The Billy Graham Center Story," http://www.wheaton.edu/bgc/bgcstory.html.

"Billy Graham New York Crusade of 1957, May 15, 1957–September 2, 1957." *Discovering U.S. History.* Gale Group, 1997, http://galenet.galegroup.com/servlet/HistRC/.

"Billy Graham's Soulmate: Life Together." *Christianity Today,* 9 July 2001, http:// www.christianitytoday.com/ct/2001/009/21.26.

Bloom, Harold. "The Preacher: Billy Graham," http://www.time.com/time/time100/heroes/profile/graham01.

Dailey, Jim. "A Conversation with George Beverly Shea." *Decision,* December 2001, http://www.billygraham.org/ourMinistries/decisionMagazine/article.asp?=104.

———. "Conversation with Ruth Bell Graham." *Decision,* May 2002, http://www.billygraham.org/ourMinistries/decisionMagazine/article.asp?=50.

Elliott, Charlotte. "Just as I Am." 1836. Reprinted in *A Victorian Anthology, 1837–1895,* edited by Edmund C. Stedman. Boston: Houghton Mifflin & Co., 1895, http://www.bartleby.com/246/324.html.

Elmore, Phil. "The Vietnam War and the American Imagination," http://philelmore.com/fiction/vietnam.htm.

Fiske, Edward B. "Billy Graham: The Closest Thing to a White House Chaplain." *The New York Times Magazine,* 8 June 1969, http://www.postitiveatheism.org/writ/graham.htm.

Fox, Frederic. "The National Day of Prayer," http://theologytoday.ptsem.edu/oct1972/v29-3-article2.htm.

Franklin Graham: Profile—The Prodigal Son Comes Home, http://www.cnn.com/CNN/Programs/people/shows/graham/profile.html.

Gilbreath, Edward. "A Conversation with Howard O. Jones." *Decision,* August 2002, http://www.billygraham.org/ourministries/decisionmagazine/article.asp?I=237.

Gitell, Seth. "Faith In the System." *Phoenix Forum,* http://www.bostonphoenix.com/boston/news_features/top/features/documents/02232943.htm.

Graham, Billy. "A Statement by Evangelist Billy Graham on Intolerance and Prejudice Following Release of Nixon White House Tapes." Press release of the BGEA, 17 March 2002, http//www.charitywire.com/00:02576.htm.

Graham, Billy. Interview by Monroe Billington. "Billy Graham Oral History." *Lyndon Baines Johnson Library Online,* 12 October 1983, http://www.lbjlib.utexas.edu/johnson/archives.hom/oral history.hom/Graham.

Jordan, Larry. "A Conversation with Billy Graham." *Midwest Today*, January 1997, http://www/,odtpd/cp,/9612/billygraham.phtml.

"Mission San Diego with Billy Graham, May 8–11, 2003, Qualcomm Stadium," http://www.jasm.org/contents/BillyGraham.htm.

" 'Only the Holy Spirit Could Have Brought It About': Interview with Dr. Billy Graham." *World Evangelization Magazine*, September 1995, http://www.gospelcom.net/lcwe/wemag/9409billyon.html.

Rowlandson, Maurice. "50 Years in Christian Work," http://www.assistnews.net/strategic/50111009.htm.

DOCUMENTS

The principal collection of documents on Billy Graham, his coworkers, and other evangelists are in the Billy Graham Center Archives at Wheaton College. A small but valuable selection of documents from the collection can be found at http://www.wheaton.edu/bgc/archives/bg.html.

INDEX

About the Author

ROGER BRUNS is an independent scholar and author of many books, including *Preacher: Billy Sunday and the Rise of American Evangelism* (1992). He has recently retired from the National Archives and Records Administration and lives in Reston, Virginia.